Murder on the Menu

JEANINE LARMOTH

MURDER
ON THE
MENU

Recipes by
Charlotte Turgeon

Charles Scribner's Sons † *New York*

For my mother

"Wait," I cried, "Don't tell me. Let me see if I can't discover it for myself."

—AGATHA CHRISTIE, *Poirot Loses a Client*

CONTENTS

INTRODUCTION

At this moment, planted throughout the world, a sinister league exists. Most members are unknown to each other until a glimpse caught on a train or an expansive moment beside a fire reveals one to another. Mystery fans. "People who [to alter the words of Lord Peter Wimsey, Dorothy Sayers's fictional detective] under ordinary circumstances are perfectly upright and amiable," but might be said to "go curly as corkscrews" when a murder is announced. Proud, haughty, singular, they select from a large body of mystery books only those which are part of the English tradition—on which the sun never sets. Somewhere in Singapore, high in the hills of Greece, cropping up in some outlandish place, as ubiquitous as the Gideon Bible, a tattered copy of Agatha Christie or Dickson Carr gives evidence that one of their number has passed.

The English mystery is more a matter of intuition than definition. It may take place in England; but it may not. Perhaps the author is English, perhaps he is not. It probably takes place in the Twenties or Thirties; but then, it might not. It will usually involve English people and characteristics long attributed to the English outlook and way of life. A fitness of things. Humor in tight places. An aura of gentility that comes of breeding and acceptance of the rules. As Julian Symons points out in "The Detective Story in Britain"; "Behind the detective story . . . there was a belief that human affairs could be ruled by reason and that virtue, generally identified with the established order of society, must prevail in the end."

Though World War II was soon, and regrettably, to destroy a way of life, and upheaval was already evident when the English mystery began its still-continuing flourish, equality had barely been acknowledged as a possibility, and had certainly not been practiced. Even where the mystery is not a definite, if unconscious, attempt to hold the line—by feeding a nostalgia for a time when modes and manners were fixed—it tries to preserve, as if in wax, a society on the verge of change. The most objective or humorous of the singularly conservative authors could not restrain a doting fondness for the pattern of a past when the sweep was of more than lawns, it was of manners.

The resulting books convey much of the grace and whimsy of civilized drawing room conversation, and reflect the values of that extremely comfortable, never taxing room. There, chintz flowers; the atmosphere is calm, but for the intrusion of death. Even that usually harsh reality is made less annoying by a titled drawing room detective who comes on the scene provided with a fitting knowledge of art and fine madeira, if not wit as well.

The most civilized mysteries gather a smart group of friends for a country weekend, flanneled for tennis, tweeded for walks, floating in pretty chiffon frocks, or suave in velvet smoking jackets. The effect is, while apparently focusing on murder, to teach a great deal about what was the fancied lot of upper class England between the wars down to the finest points of social usage. As a result, these books have become perfect records, not just of social dreams, but the attitudes that formed them.

Class distinctions are presented without a blush. The gentry are so clearly the gentry that a lower servant automatically bobs, even when a gentleman's name and rank are entirely unknown to him. Likewise, a gentleman resents familiarity offered him by an unknown of lower class on the grounds that it should be evident what he is. It is as possible to identify members of different classes, simply by sight, as it is to distinguish travelers from another country.

The reader is as familiar with the system and the setting as are the characters, from the accumulated lore, built stone on stone, timber by timber, teacup after teacup by a league of industrious authors. There is no need to mention more than a few phrases— "big hall," "bounder," "arranging flowers," "the butler's pantry"—for the reader to be on his way, daubing in the glint of silver in a darkened cupboard, adding a drooping dahlia, a twinkling prism from out of his own vast stores of reading.

Strange as it seems to consider books devoted to murder nonviolent, they are. Murders rarely number more than three, are minimally described and, except as a necessary part of theory, relegated to the background after they occur. Intrigue, tension, the chase are kept at decorous, just-titillating levels. Danger is contained. If the crime is ostensibly caused by emotion, even the privacy of a book is too open for revelation. The classic English mystery may be romantic but, like the classic Western, it is sexless.

At its best, the mystery is a puzzle of character or possibility; a fairytale, somewhat sharpened, pulled down to earth. Its witches are more recognizable, its pattern familiar, but its outcome unknown. Like the fairytale, it is frightening enough to make the bedcovers snugger, light warmer, and indoors nicer, as it is on a rainy night. Like fairyland, the mystery is portable: a soothing, predictable world packed in your pocket to unfurl like a patchwork quilt covering strange places and times in dear familiarity.

In presenting this world, many of the outstanding exponents of mystery writing picked and chose the rules they intended to follow from among those established for the genre. Among the original Thou Shalt Nots were: a surprise twin, Chinamen, undiscovered poisons, supernatural explanations, or concealed clues; they limited secret panels to one, required the criminal to be mentioned early on, the detective to have crime-free hands, and the detective's alter ego to reveal his innermost thoughts. Fitful adherents wrote books in which the narrator turns out to be the murderer, the murderer is a ten-year-old girl, there hasn't been a murder, or the murder was as communally committed as the slaughter of Caesar.

But no matter how the writers darted and dodged, one rule remained sacrosanct. The rule of the table. The author might diddle the reader and hide the clues, but never did he or she toy with the finer sensibilities of the characters' stomachs. The respect for their stomachs is, in fact, more acute than the respect for their lives.

After a murder ends a life and disrupts a household, there is no question of grabbing a sandwich or forgetting to eat altogether. The murder mystery, like a good army, marches on its stomach. No sooner are the reader's senses keyed to a clue than there is a clatter of dishes, a reassuring aroma in the air, and luncheon is served. The description that inevitably follows is so loving, you rise unconsciously and make your way to your own kitchen.

While making a case for the mystery as a social record, G. C. Ramsey, author of *Agatha Christie, Mistress of Mystery,* wistfully reveals himself as just such a victim of his author's culinary wiles: "It is true that the world will not rise or fall on the matter of a lace fichu (or a shift), but if future historians wish to find out how breakfast was served in English country houses after World War I, they will get more information and background about the system in operation from *The Secret of Chimneys* and *The Seven Dials Mystery* than any cookery book or historical text can provide. For this reason, it is wise not to read Agatha Christie late at night if one is dieting. After a particularly mouth-watering breakfast or luncheon scene, one is apt to think, 'You know, it would be rather fun if I could do that.'"

Murder on the Menu fills in the gaps between description and dish by supplying recipes for those ingredients of which mystery books are made. Recipes described or implied in mouth-watering opera from Dorothy Sayers' *Strong Poison* to Agatha Christie's *Funerals Are Fatal*. The recipes are for food which would be served in English homes. But this, of course, goes well beyond roast beef and Yorkshire pudding. English cuisine comes from every region where the British flag has waved, an English ship put in, or Poirot has set his high-buttoned boot. The result is, like the British themselves, a worldly and at-ease cuisine. The recipes are serious. This cookbook is meant to amuse, stimulate, and succor the insatiable appetite of the ever-hungry mystery reader.

Thus, when night falls, the reader can sink his tastebuds in atmosphere—recollections of a well-cooked meal, a mystery book in hand. One is always extra snug reading a mystery; the covers feel cosier, the pillow plumper. What ho! Is this a cup of chocolate by the bed? Ah, so much the better.

Murder
in the
Country

ONE

The Lay of the Land

The corpse must shock not only because it is a corpse but also because, even for a corpse, it is shockingly out of place. . . .

W. H. AUDEN, "The Guilty Vicarage"

A mystery is a land where the snow never melts, and the ground is always a little muddy for footprints. Where bushes grow to have their twigs snapped by a murderer, and to drink deeply is to die of poison.

The best murders take place at only the best places. A first-class compartment on a crack train, a chic Cadogan Square address, an opulent hotel in Egypt. But the most pleasurable of all, because the most remote from reality, yet nearest the remembered land of fairy tales, is the country house. Of all the backgrounds it provides the largest canvas: a grand gesture of land, the rumblings and innuendos of nature, a clearing in the midst of civilization for the interplay of character.

The soft beauty of the English countryside, its green sweeps and dappled meadows, its haze and winding streams, the bucolic innocence it presents to the eye, sharpen the cruel contrast of murder. Every flutter of a leaf, every dot of color in the landscape, every swipe of the butler's cloth, the hearty laugh of the Tweedy Lady, a collie gone to Victorian plumpness, heighten the tenuous and delicious balance between security and insecurity, make the knife stroke sharper, the ring of a shot more jarring. By lulling us, beauty makes the horror more shocking. How can murder occur bedded in harebells and white violets, sweetened by the scent of hay? But even behind that bristling hedge, it waits.

Around us is a Sleeping Beauty world, a land of nightmares come true, ominously asleep, nodding behind thickets of rhododendron, while chandeliers glitter, and the air is pungent with the scent of wax polish, roses, and potpourri.

Within the house, the beauty of the countryside is transformed to a perfected way of life. The skies are no softer than the linens; the hills no more elegant than the fluted panels of the drawing room. Everything evidences all that is most precious in the English way of life. The art of artlessness. The glory of effortlessness. The assumption of rightness, a modesty of manner, unspoken rules of conduct, a recognition of order, unquestioned, unexamined, accepted. By every member of the household, by all members of the society beyond. World without end.

A country whose love of restraint is so great a command is unspoken is not a country of crisp edges or the ostentatiously new. The arms of the chintz chairs must be worn, even a bit smudgy (possibly, having been used in the servants' hall first); the drapes are faded. Heavy-headed roses are surrounded by soft splashes of fallen petals on the table. Even the correct order of the garden is disorder. Flowers tumble close to the ground, tousled as if they had slept badly; lean lazily, or shoot into the air with the gleeful and riotous disorder of a winning team of cricketers.

Beyond the walls, everyone is presumed comfortably off or,

at any rate, content with his lot; not restive or ambitious, not likely to cause trouble, not likely to upset the smooth-rolling apple cart.

It is a world too solid for anything to go wrong. And yet, it does.

Behind the house, the canvas stretches as far as the eye can see. But, though smoke may curl from the chimneys just beyond the rise, the occupants will never drop by for a glass of Madeira and Madeira cake in the morning. The house party is isolated; as cut off in fair weather as in foul. The great house stands alone, a sumptuous dwelling from our dreams, singled out for the wrathful spectacle of murder.

TWO

Murder on the House

> . . . the good detective story is in its nature of good domestic story. It is steeped in the sentiment that the Englishman's house is his castle; even if, like other castles, it is the scene of a few quiet tortures or assassinations.
>
> G. K. CHESTERTON, "The Domesticity of the Detective"

Despite the modest name, suitable for something shabby where one cooks on a gas ring, the country house is usually more on the scale of Blenheim Palace; whether late-Georgian or early-Tudor pile, there is an east and a west wing. The sporting facilities outstrip a country club's; the service is more polished than the finest hotel's. A park with a small lake for punting, bowling and croquet lawns, terraces, gardens, hothouses, stables, long barns and short, forests, chicken coops, gardener's sheds, caretaker's lodges, lightly balanced urns on the balustrades, wait the selection of the most discriminating murderer.

Though all the grounds seem made for murder, some murderers prefer not to get their feet wet. Therefore, it falls on certain rooms to be chosen for the event, some with a great deal more frequency than others. Because of this, it is possible to predict with a fair degree of accuracy where murders will take place, and where they will not.

The kitchen, for example. The kitchen is a sacred preserve; the safest room in the house. When someone cries havoc, it's the best place to run. There is a tacit understanding among author, guests, servants, victims, and murderer: no crime in the kitchen. The murderer may come to borrow a knife, but not to carve; to diddle the dinner, but not make mincemeat. The reason is operational. Too off-putting. Sagging appetites, frittering nerves. As one must keep up one's strength, one isn't going to attack the headquarters, the very bastion of strengthening, thus stopping soups mid-bubble, chilling glowing fires, cooling the tea kettle. No one could, no one would put the kitchen out of commission. Not even a grudgeful Nanny who has it in for the cook. And a mass invasion of the kitchen by the police would put the cook in such a state she couldn't boil an egg, much less prepare the meal everyone's looking forward to.

The dining room is less sacred, but safe by association. People prefer not to step over a corpse on the way to breakfast. Dampens the appetite. Opens the mind to unnecessary metaphysical speculations (and we know how we feel about that. See Chapter 19, "The Vicar"). It could be days before the police finish photographing, hunting fingerprints, etc. In cases of poisoning, however, dining rooms are rather often employed.

The drawing room falls between. If murder must be done, one must make do, but the drawing room is so cheery a place, and so dear to the heart of the family most murderers respectfully circumvent it. The wood-paneled walls, the side tables and their tea caddies, the chairs embellished with gros point, the chintz and antique tapestries, provide a gentle air of order. Magazines with pictures of hunting dogs, landscapes, or advertisements like handbills on the covers lie scattered about, suitably dog-eared and out-of-date. Through the French windows, the flowers of the season mix with the odor of burning logs, the fresh, sweet scent of tea, or pipe tobacco. In summer, roses blend with the moonlight; the piercing perfume of chrysanthemums echoes the pale moonlight of autumn. Even the fender is more appropriate for toasting chestnuts or crumpets than supporting a lolling head. The library is infinitely more suitable.

Most crimes of violence occur in libraries after ten o'clock at night. The library of an English home is an arena second only to the Colosseum in mortality rate; it is set aside for no other purpose than killing. Unlike the drawing room, the library can get over murder handily. It is both unworldly and impersonal enough to be impervious to the encroachments of the present: the atmosphere of timelessness helps minimize the nastiness of the moment. In a bedroom, murders are invariably under cover, masked as suicide or natural causes. In the library, the murderer doesn't care who knows it. Traffic is light, so he has a fair chance to work uninterrupted (and should he be, there are always the plum-colored velvet drapes to hide behind). No room is better implemented with all the murderous necessaries so impossible to pack. There are pokers, andirons, paperweights, and decanters for thwacks; typewriters, clocks, and inkpots for clues. A grate lies ready to hand to devour incriminating notes, gloves, and plimsolls; the hearthrug to receive the latest lifeless form.

Heads roll on the desk with a regularity the guillotine never enjoyed. They are used like bowling balls to dislodge pots of ink which, gushing, succeed in just about totally eliminating a note— authentic or forged—that lies under a dead hand. If the note is rendered virtually unreadable by ink or fire, it has a fair chance of authenticity. If legible, it is a fraud. A blotter lies ready to give a reverse reading of some premurder jottings, and a typewriter to give a clue by its peculiarity in striking the letter "o." Clocks tick all their days toward the moment when they will be knocked off the desk to give an exact accounting of the time of the murder or, more often, the time the murderer has selected to appear to be the time of the murder.

No man should go into the library unaccompanied, particularly if he plans to write a note. If he hasn't an enemy in the world, one will appear. And there he'll be, head lolling by the inkpot. Pen fallen to the floor. It just isn't safe for a man to write notes. He should wire instead.

Should the murderer wish to attempt to divert suspicion from the household, the French doors may be left ajar with drapes flapping, and a bit of snow traced on the carpet to make it appear the murderer came in from the outside. Or the door of the safe can hang open to reveal a depleted supply of heavy ropes of pearls, if he wishes to make it seem the motive was robbery. While he's there, the thoughtful murderer removes the will which makes him the heir, in order to point the suspicion at someone else.

Staircases are hardly less hazardous than libraries, especially for the general public. It is amazing how important staircases are altogether. They are a sociological divider. People get lower or higher by going up or down them. There are different levels, and different meanings for different levels. A top floor in Mayfair overlooking Hyde Park is not the same as a top floor in Tottenham Court Road. In a great house, those who live Above Stairs are not the same as those who live Below. Therefore, stairs are needed to keep people in their places.

Apart from the sociological, however, stairs have a direct application in crime. Not so much for victims to be pushed down, as for them to be found sprawled on like discarded fur tippets. There is something special about waking in the night to hear a thump, bump, bump that cannot be the biggest feet or largest ball going down the steps. Similarly, it will seem very special to the maid, coming up the stairs in the morning with the breakfast trays, when she trips over Something, and lets trays fly, raining knives, spoons, and marmalade over the hall below. Since, out of deference, everyone else is outside hanging on the ivy, the murderer has the staircase pretty much all to himself when he wants to slip down to the library and doctor the spirits, or give the sandwiches an extra tang.

† THE LIBRARY SNACK

The library snack is left on a small table by the butler, after he has locked the doors and windows, and before he retires at eleven. The snack is meant for the late arrival of the master of the house, but the murderer may put it to other uses. For the pacific mystery reader, a library snack is excellent for the cocktail hour. But beware those tempting tidbits. Still, they do look good, don't they? Perhaps I will . . . just one. And, oh, a little one.

LIBRARY SNACKS *(What waits beside the whisky)*
> Soufflé Sardine Canapés
> Scotch Salmon Toasts
> Chutney Canapés
> Apple Cheddar Open Sandwiches
> Angels on Horseback
> Devils on Horseback
> Scotch Eggs
> Cornish Pasties
> Anchovy Stuffed Eggs
> Scotch Oatcakes
> Potted Shrimp

† SOUFFLÉ SARDINE CANAPÉS

1 can boneless, skinless sardines
1 tbsp mayonnaise
½ tsp sharp, prepared mustard

½ tsp grated onion
1 egg white, beaten stiff
toast or Melba toast

Preheat the oven to 400° F. Crush the sardines with a fork. Mix thoroughly with the mayonnaise, mustard, and onion. Fold in the egg white and spread on 8 thin slices of toast or packaged Melba toast, or on 16 small Melba toast rounds. Place on a baking sheet and bake 8 minutes. Serve immediately.

† SCOTCH SALMON TOASTS

Toast and butter thin slices of whole wheat or white bread. Cover each one generously with overlapping slices of smoked salmon. Dot with bits of fresh lemon and sprinkle with chopped parsley.

† CHUTNEY CANAPÉS

Place a piece of chutney on each Melba toast round. Cover with rounds of Muenster cheese and bake in a 425° F oven until the cheese melts.

† APPLE CHEDDAR OPEN SANDWICHES

Spread slices of whole wheat bread lightly with butter and Dijon-type mustard. Peel, core and slice apples as you would for a pie. Lay several slices on each piece of bread. Sprinkle with chopped walnuts and cover with a slice of sharp Cheddar cheese. Bake at 425° F until the cheese melts.

† ANGELS ON HORSEBACK

These make an excellent accompaniment to cocktails, and they may also be served as a first course, or as a savory at the end of a meal. Serve on hot, buttered toast (2 per serving).

Take shucked oysters and wrap each in a half slice of bacon secured with a small skewer or toothpick. Bake at 450° F for 5 to 8 minutes or until the bacon is done.

† DEVILS ON HORSEBACK

Soak 12 prunes in boiling water for 30 minutes. Drain them and dry on a paper towel. Remove the stones. Stuff them with chutney and wrap each in a half slice of bacon, secured with a small skewer or toothpick. Bake at 450° F for 5 to 8 minutes or until the bacon is done.

† SCOTCH EGGS

8 eggs	1 tsp water
1½ lbs sausage meat	fine bread crumbs
1 egg yolk	vegetable shortening

Hardboil the eggs, shell them, and let them cool thoroughly. Be sure they are perfectly dry.

Divide the sausage meat into 8 portions, and flatten each portion with the palm of your hand. Wrap each egg in a thin coat of the sausage meat, making sure that each egg is entirely covered. Blend the egg yolk with the water, and spread the bread crumbs on a plate. Dip each egg in the egg yolk and then in the crumbs. Let them stand for at least 30 minutes in the refrigerator.

Heat enough shortening in a frying pan to measure ¾ of an inch deep. The fat should be hot (325° F), but not so hot as to burn the sausage meat. Brown the eggs on all sides and drain on paper towels.

These may be served either hot or cold. When they are served cold, cut them in half for a delicious accompaniment to a pint of beer, or serve as a hearty hors d'oeuvre with cocktails.

† CORNISH PASTIES

Savory Pie Pastry (see page 261)
½ lb beef steak
3 lamb kidneys
2 medium potatoes
1 onion
1 carrot

1 tbsp chopped parsley
½ tsp seasoned salt
⅛ tsp nutmeg
pepper
1 egg yolk blended with
1 tsp water

Make a double recipe of the pie pastry and let it rest while making the filling.

Trim the steak and kidneys and dice them very fine. Peel and dice the vegetables equally fine, and drop them into boiling water for 1 minute. Drain them and combine them with the meat. Mix with the parsley and seasonings. The mixture should be highly seasoned. Cool thoroughly.

Preheat the oven to 375° F.

Roll out the pastry ⅛ inch thick, and cut it in 3 inch rounds. Brush the edge of half the rounds with a little cold water. Place 1 tsp of the mixture on the center of the moistened rounds and cover with the remaining pastry rounds, pinching the edges firmly together. Place on a baking sheet. Prick each pastry with a fork and paint with the egg yolk blended with the water. Bake 30 minutes. This will make 24 pasties which may be served immediately or reheated later.

† ANCHOVY STUFFED EGGS

8 eggs	1 tsp anchovy paste
3 tbsp unsalted butter	anchovy fillets
	parsley

Simmer the eggs for 12 minutes. Drain, crack the shells. Cool. Peel and halve the eggs lengthwise. Remove the yolks and mash them with the butter and the anchovy paste. Fill the whites either by forcing the yolk mixture through a pastry tube or with a spoon. Crisscross each half with thin strips of anchovy fillets and garnish with a sprig of parsley.

† SCOTCH OATCAKES

1 cup oatmeal	2 tsp vegetable oil
¼ tsp salt	½ cup boiling water
½ tsp baking soda	butter

Combine the oatmeal, salt, and baking soda. Add the vegetable oil and enough hot water to make a stiff dough. Sprinkle the working surface with oatmeal and knead the dough until a thick, elastic ball is formed. Roll out ¼ inch thick and cut into rounds with a 2½-inch cookie cutter.

Heat a large, heavy skillet or a Teflon-lined frying pan. Press oatmeal into one side of each round, and place them coated side down in the moderately hot skillet. Cook about 5 minutes or until a toasty brown on the bottom. With a spatula, turn them over onto a baking sheet. Press more oatmeal onto the uncoated side, and toast them under the broiler until lightly brown. Spread with butter and serve with cheese and ale.

† *POTTED SHRIMP*

3 tbsp butter	½ tsp anchovy paste
1 tsp finely chopped shallots	½ lb small shrimp, cooked and
¼ tsp mace	cleaned
½ tsp freshly ground pepper	2 tbsp hot clarified butter

Heat the butter over low heat. Sauté the shallots until soft. Stir in the mace, pepper, and anchovy paste. Add the shrimp and cook gently for 3 minutes, stirring frequently. Put the shrimps in two small pots, pressing them down. When cool cover with the clarified butter. Cool completely. Cover with aluminum foil and refrigerate. These will keep for weeks. Serve with crisp toast.

THREE

Strong Drink

There was a crash of falling glass. Alec Portal, helping himself to whisky, had let the decanter slip. "I say—damn' sorry.
Can't think what came over me."

ACATHA CHRISTIE, "The Coming of Mr. Quin"

Drink has been a staple of the British Empire. India was built
on gin and pith helmets. Whisky tells us, as clearly as waving a
Union Jack or singing "God Save the Queen," that we are in
England, and in the company of civilized (if for the moment
erring) men. It also serves to keep the weather out, a kind of
brolly over the spirits. That such a stanchion should be a major
support of the mystery is hardly surprising. At the club or in the
drawing room, the soft gurgle as it pours soothes out a story or
two, and gives a suspiciously agitated guest an opportunity to almost crush a glass in his hand, thus raising questions in another

guest's mind. As clothes reveal the man, too much whisky reveals the blighter; his weakness or guilt.

The possibilities for a beautifully cut crystal decanter are multiple. It can, of course, simply glitter in library or drawing room adding, with the siphon and whisky bottle, the convivial atmosphere implicit in a drink in the gathering shadows of late afternoon by a newly laid fire. It can also be used for more ominous purposes. It can hold port, and the port can hold strychnine. Or, to tell the brutal truth, decanters can be handy to bash someone's head in. Then, should another guest be taken faint on viewing, he may be offered a drink, thus killing two birds with one decanter.

The presence of the seltzer bottle, by promising the coming of whisky, is as welcome as the sign swaying over an inn door. Seltzer bottles sit on the drink trolley where they are rolled in by the butler every evening at six, whether or not anyone is in the drawing room. That way, drinks are readily accessible to the house guests, or any passerby just in through the French doors. A seltzer bottle is a truly noble instrument. It brings order in the drawing room, as surely as does a mace into the courtroom. It is so valued that Carter Dickson's august Sir Henry Merrivale keeps his in a safe. It would be a fine thing to see the seltzer bottle replace the crown as the insignia on mail vans.

There are three categories of drink in mysteries: strong, civilized, and refined. Whisky and gin are in the first category. In the second, the wines of France and Germany, the tawny port of pub lunches, the after-dinner port of cigars and ladies-in-another-room; and sherry, which even ladies may have with biscuits in the afternoon. In the third group are the homemade brews made from receipts passed on, sanctified, from grandmothers twice removed, so that even a spinster who has seen too much may have some and, after a tipple, be off and running like a filly.

All drinks in mystery books are means of introduction—of poison, not people. It is up to you to reverse such an inhospitable trend, and introduce not just a new group of people, but a group of new drinks to people.

STRONG DRINKS
> *Irish Coffee*
> *Hot Grog*
> *Hot Gin Sling*
> *Milk Posset*
> *Syllabub*
> *Mulled Wine*
> *Gin and It*
> *Black Velvet*
> *Pimm's Cup*
> *Pink Gin*
> *Atholl Brose*

† *IRISH COFFEE*
for each serving

1½ oz Irish whisky	⅔ cup freshly brewed strong coffee
1 tbsp Grand Marnier	1 tbsp chilled very heavy cream
1 tsp sugar	

Rinse out a heavy goblet in very hot water and shake it dry. Stir The whisky, Grand Marnier, and sugar in the glass until the sugar dissolves. Add the hot coffee. Carefully pour the cream over a silver spoon onto the coffee so that it floats. Serve immediately.

† HOT GROG
(for each serving)

2 oz rum   boiling water
1 tbsp lemon juice   1 slice lemon
1 tsp sugar

Combine the rum, lemon juice, and sugar in a heavy goblet. Stir and add the boiling water. Garnish with a slice of lemon.

† HOT GIN SLING
(for each serving)

2 oz gin   boiling water
1 tsp sugar

Place the gin and sugar in a heavy prewarmed goblet. Fill with boiling water.

† MILK POSSET
(2 servings)

2 cups milk   6 tsp sugar
½ cup dry white wine   nutmeg

Boil the milk and wine until the mixture separates. Strain into a serving bowl and add the sugar and a dusting of nutmeg.

† *SYLLABUB*
(2 to 3 servings)

2 cups medium cream	juice of 2 lemons
1 cup Bristol Cream Sherry	sugar
	nutmeg

Beat all the ingredients except nutmeg together in a bowl until the mixture is frothy. Sweeten to taste. Serve with a dusting of nutmeg.

† *MULLED WINE*
(4 to 6 servings)

½ tsp ground cloves	2 cups water
½ tsp cinnamon	1 bottle red Bordeaux wine
½ tsp nutmeg	sugar

Boil the spices in the water in a covered saucepan for 5 minutes. Add the wine and 1 tbsp sugar. Bring almost to a boil and taste for sweetening, adding more sugar if desired.

Cider or other wines may be used instead of the red Bordeaux.

† *GIN AND IT*
(for each serving)

$\frac{2}{3}$ gin
$\frac{1}{3}$ sweet vermouth

Shake well with ice before serving.

† *BLACK VELVET*
(for each serving)

½ champagne
½ Guinness stout

Pour well-chilled champagne and stout into large goblets and serve immediately.

† *PIMM'S CUP*
(for each serving)

1½ oz Pimm's Cup No. 1   cucumber
lemon soda or Tom Collins mix   borage or mint

Pour the Pimm's Cup over ice in an old-fashioned glass. Fill with the soda and garnish with a thin strip of cucumber rind and a sprig of borage or mint.

† *PINK GIN*
(for each serving)

Put 2 or 3 drops of Angostura bitters in an old-fashioned glass and swirl it around to coat the sides. Pour in 1½ oz or more of gin. Add approximately the same amount of water and ice. Serve very cold.

† *ATHOLL BROSE*
   (4 to 6 servings)

3 cups old-fashion oatmeal   10 tbsp cream
1¼ cups cold water·   4 tbsp strained honey
10 tbsp Drambuie

Put the oatmeal in a bowl and stir in the water. Set aside for at least an hour. Strain, pressing the oatmeal to extract the water until the liquid measures 10 tbsp. Mix in the Drambuie, cream, and honey. Serve in wine glasses.

FOUR

Those Who Live in Glass Houses

"Quite right," said Peter, "when I hear people movin' about
the house at night, I'm much too delicate-minded to think
anything at all."

"Of course," interposed the Duchess, "particularly in
England, where it is so oddly improper to think."

DOROTHY L. SAYERS, *Clouds of Witness*

Of all the ways to organize a murder, the country weekend is the
best. Not only is the setting verdant and serene, all the best
people attend them: aristocrats, and old county families, whose
bloodlines will only be refreshed by a little bloodletting. Everyone is known to everyone else, if not from birth, by breeding.

No group of people is better organized for murder. All the
unwritten rules that guide social conduct have long since been
agreed upon, so that the single act of murder is isolated against
a background of stability. Everyone but the murderer is harmo-
niously fixed in his setting as the house is on its grounds. The

position of those in the party is assured, and assumed without need to contrast it with the outside world. They are upper class, therefore disinterested, therefore we may rely on them. They are above petty considerations and the need for them. Should the wolf appear at the door, they would think it a fox in disguise just strayed from the hunt. They must, apart from murder, live a life of order and plenty, and be impervious to minor disasters. As there is no code for proper behavior after a murder, it will be treated much as if it were an outcropping of a lesser social aberration to be kept down, like all the rest of them. If possible, the guests would prefer to ignore it altogether. When they hear a shot, they tell themselves it's a poacher. When faced with the body, they argue for suicide, even though for the victim to be shot or stabbed at that particular angle would have necessitated that he have an arm on backward.

The hosts of the house party are the Admirable Eccentric, the Flighty Daughter, and the Dotty Duchess—providing she can absent herself from a War of the Roses with the gardener long enough to come to the tea table. The members of the house party are friends or family who have motored down for the weekend, or gone to Yorkshire for a longer period at a shooting box.

Suitable young men are invited to house parties by the Admirable Eccentric and his wife who seem, despite the inconvenience—the young men's late arrival at breakfast or failure to come down at all because they are dead in bed—to like nothing better than having them about. In return for the hospitality, the young men apologize with engaging frankness, while wolfing down toast and marmalade, for being late, look over the girls, play bridge with the host, and listen to the hostess's complaints about the gardener with a sympathetic air. Between weekends, they have jobs at the Foreign Office, where they arrive at eleven. In town, they have rooms in Jermyn Street, where they are looked after by a former butler and his wife.

Sometimes, the young man is American. Nice Americans,

when encountered, always resemble cub reporters—brash, but endearing. Apparently they have fallen from some Ivy League college, through a Ben Hecht net, and have floated to England on a wave of jazz, no matter where they came from or what they were doing there. Generally, such an American does not commit murders. He is too much of an innocent for that: it might hurt his freckles. But neither may he aspire to Lady Daphne's hand, unless she is one of those frightfully modern gels one can do nothing with, and who is bound to be disinherited anyway. Then she might as well marry an American. The butler will hang himself in the larder from chagrin either way.

When it occurs on such a weekend, murder will be an annoyance. Nothing more elaborate was planned than billiards and bridge, tennis and piquet, and walks in the woods to work up an appetite for the next meal. However, at the sound of a Malacca cane—marked in inches, compass on top, and sword inside—rattling into the umbrella stand, a sigh of relief will go up. The aristocratic detective cometh. A man of one's own kind to the rescue. The enclosed world may stay enclosed. So much less awkward, don't y'know.

FIVE

Tea Service: The Ritual of Tea

A bright idea came into Alice's head. "Is that the reason so many tea-things are put out here?" she asked.

"Yes, that's it," said the Hatter with a sigh. "It's always tea-time, and we've no time to wash the things between whiles."

"Then you keep moving round, I suppose?" said Alice.

"Exactly so," said the Hatter; "as the things get used up."

"But what happens when you come to the beginning again?" Alice ventured to ask.

LEWIS CARROLL, *Alice's Adventures in Wonderland*

It is always time for tea in a mystery. You may plummet out of the sky and into a cabbage patch, and still be in time for tea. After thirty years in India, as you crested the knoll of the hill, you would see the family, just as you left it, pouring tea. Looking up, the hostess remarks, "Oh, I say! Jolly good! One lump or two?" Nor can you refuse, no matter how many cups you've already had, unless you want to watch your hostess's face pucker

like the skin on cooling cocoa. For it soothes a woman's maternal
instincts to see you enjoying your tea.

There is a marvelous sense of isolation about the tea table,
rocking easily as a peagreen boat in the midst of a green sea of
lawn that runs down to the ha-ha. The beech trees rustle. The
wrens chirp. A body lies, as if drowsing, in a copse of birch and
azaleas. Even the tinkling of a little silver bell that summons the
shuffling butler from dozing in the pantry cannot break the
spell. All is most assuredly right with the world.

Tea at the Great House is well-mannered. In times of stress
it is the way the guests pull themselves together. But, unlike a
proper or high tea, which is merely a question of substance
and starch, tea cannot be a spontaneous eruption like a mushroom on the lawn to succor the fainting. That's for the kitchen,
and the working classes. The upper classes must hold up, while
things are done properly: the servants set up the ancient
colored umbrella and wicker table on the lawn, and Old Dodders rolls out the trolley laden with silver tea equipage, and
the bread-and-butter sandwiches layered with cucumbers, rose
petals, or nasturtium leaves. Once this has been accomplished,
and after a brief shower has forced everyone back into the
house for an hour, tea will be served. The young ladies of the
house party, smoothing their light frocks, spring up around the
table, so many charming crocuses. As a result of not yielding
to the pressures of the moment, of refusing to acknowledge
emergencies, the upper classes don't faint as often as the lower.
Discipline, my dear, discipline.

Domestic calm is no better seen than at the tea table on a
murderous weekend. A spot of murder never hurt anything.
True, as she serves, the hostess is unaware of the somewhat irregular behavior of one of her guests resting in the bushes. But
did she know, we may be sure, she would continue pouring, and
never splash a drop. Tradition has that effect on people. The
concern of the Dotty Duchess is for the state of the milk jug, the
fruit cake, and the whereabouts of the staff.

Of all the arts cultivated by the English, none is more enviable than this ease, the sense of the fitness of things, an unagitated harboring of the homely pleasures, and a determination to see them continued, no matter where, no matter what the circumstances.

While the stone walls of the Great House represent the external solidity, the characters represent the internal solidity of an unchanging society, and supposed upper class values. The expected response must come to a given situation, as predictably as the butler answering the tinkling of the bell. Ritual must be observed, for ritual represents the eternalized moment, the fixed moment in a fixed society. By pouring tea day after day, we assure ourselves that we always will; that there'll always be a we, always be tea, and always be an England.

† THE TEA TROLLEY

Tea

TEA SANDWICHES

Asparagus Rolls

Mustard Beef Sandwiches

Watercress Sandwiches

Anchovy Rolls

Roe Sandwiches

Crumpets

Tongue Paste Sandwiches

Potted Cheese and Biscuits

Mrs. Appelbee's Pressed Meat

Bread and Butter

Lemon Curd Tartlets

Cream Scones

Lancaster Treacle Parkin

English Loaf Cake

Lemon Sponge Roll
Seed Cake
Cornish Saffron Bread
Scotch Shortbread

† ASPARAGUS ROLLS

Parboil thin asparagus stalks for 2 minutes. Plunge immediately into cold water. Remove the crusts from thin-sliced white bread. Spread with a thin film of butter and then with well-seasoned mayonnaise. Lay an asparagus stalk cut long enough to fill the sandwich and leave the tip showing. Roll up the bread around the asparagus and fasten with a toothpick. Chill in the refrigerator. Remove the toothpick before serving.

† MUSTARD BEEF SANDWICHES

Mix Bahamian or Dijon mustard with homemade or unspiced mayonnaise in the proportion of 1½ tsp of mustard to ½ cup of mayonnaise. Spread on slices of firm white bread from which the crusts have been removed. Cover half of them with a generous portion of *thinly* sliced roast beef and sprinkle with salt and pepper. Cover with the remaining slices of bread and press firmly together before cutting them in triangles.

† WATERCRESS SANDWICHES

Wash thoroughly watercress leaves stripped from their stems and chop them very fine. Mix with whipped butter in the proportion of ¼ cup of leaves to 6 tbsp butter. Season with salt, black pepper, and lemon juice. Spread between thin slices of firm white bread and cut into fingers.

† *ANCHOVY ROLLS*

Buy soft miniature-size rolls, no larger than a silver dollar. Mix anchovy paste and unsalted butter in the proportion of 1 tsp anchovy paste to 4 tbsp butter. Spread lavishly between split halves of rolls.

† *ROE SANDWICHES*

Mix the contents of a 12-oz can of shad roe with ¼ lb butter or use 1 cup of fresh, cooked fish roe. Season with 1 tsp grated onion, 2 tsp finely chopped parsley, salt, white pepper, and a little lemon juice. Mix well and spread between thin slices of white or wholewheat bread.

† *CRUMPETS*

4½ cups all-purpose flour	1 tsp sugar
1½ tsp salt	½ cup lukewarm water
2 packages dry yeast	1 quart nonfat milk

Place the flour and salt in a pan and warm in a moderate oven for about 5 minutes. Dissolve the yeast and sugar in the water. Heat the milk to lukewarm. Combine with the yeast mixture. Put the flour and salt in a mixing bowl and add the milk and yeast mixture gradually, beating until all is fairly smooth and rather liquid. Cover and let rise at room temperature for 45 minutes.

Butter a heavy skillet or griddle and place on it 6 well buttered crumpet rings. (Satisfactory rings may be made by cutting out the tops and bottoms of 7 oz tin cans about 3 inches in diameter.) Heat thoroughly on the top of the stove. Fill the rings about half full with the batter and cook 10 minutes over moderately high heat (375° F). Remove the rings with a pair of tongs and turn the crumpets over. Brown for another 6 minutes. Repeat the process 3 more times. Serve the crumpets buttered and toasted on one side, or split, buttered and toasted. Crumpets may be frozen and used later.

These resemble English muffins which are made in the same way but with a stiffer dough. Use 3 cups of milk instead of a quart and add ½ cup flour to produce a dough that can be shaped with well-floured hands.

† *TONGUE PASTE SANDWICHES*

Mix ground cooked tongue with soft butter in the proportion of 1 cup of tongue to ½ cup of butter. Mix well with a fork and add the yolks of 2 hard-cooked eggs and season with mayonnaise, horseradish, salt, and pepper. Spread between thin slices of rye or pumpernickel bread. Press together, remove the crusts, and cut in squares.

† *POTTED CHEESE AND BISCUITS*

Cut ½ lb of sharp Cheddar cheese in small pieces or grate it. Mash with 3 tbsp butter, 2 to 3 tbsp madeira, and a pinch of nutmeg. Work into a smooth paste and put it in a covered pot. Store in the refrigerator for at least a day before using. Put it on a small tray and surround it with water wafers, split and toasted under the broiler.

† *MRS. APPELBEE'S PRESSED MEAT*

1½ lbs loin of pork	1 tsp salt
1 lb chuck beef	⅓ tsp pepper

Put the meat in a kettle and add enough water to just cover. Add the salt and pepper and boil gently for 2½ to 3 hours or until the bones fall away from the pork. Remove the meat from the liquid and boil down the liquid until it measures about 1¼ cups. Strain.

When the meat is cool enough to handle, force it through a meat grinder and place it in a loaf tin. Slowly add the reduced liquid. Season to taste with salt and pepper. It should be quite moist. Cover with another tin and weight it down with some heavy object. Chill in the refrigerator. This is excellent sandwich material.

† BREAD AND BUTTER

Fresh butter spread on fresh bread, preferably homemade, is ambrosial and very suitable for tea. For variations, flavor the butter with freshly chopped herbs—chives, parsley, basil, tarragon, or chervil —or a little grated onion, salt and black pepper, or anchovy paste.

† LEMON CURD TARTLETS

Two Crust Dessert Pastry (page 260)   1 cup sugar
6 tbsp butter   3 eggs, beaten well
2 lemons, grated rind and juice

Make the pastry and let it rest. Melt the butter in the top part of a double boiler and add the rest of the ingredients. Stir constantly over simmering water to prevent the bottom and sides of the pan from becoming coated. The mixture will thicken in about 5 to 6 minutes. Pour immediately into a bowl and cool before covering. This curd will keep for a long time in the refrigerator.

Roll out the pastry ¼ inch thick. Cut in 4 inch circles. Line individual tin or aluminum tartlet pans with the circles, pressing into place with your fingers. Prick the pastry in several places. Chill for a half hour or more.

Cover the pastry with aluminum foil and weight it down with dried beans to keep it from rising. Bake 10 minutes at 425° F. Remove the beans and foil and continue baking 4 to 5 minutes or until golden brown. Remove from the oven and slip the tartlets from the tins. Cool before filling with the curd.

† CREAM SCONES

2½ cups all-purpose flour	½ tsp salt
¼ tsp cream of tartar	4 tbsp butter
½ tsp baking soda	¾ cup light cream
2 tsp sugar	

Preheat the oven to 450° F.

Sift the dry ingredients into a bowl. Blend in butter with a fork. Add cream, stirring quickly, until the dough is soft but not sticky. Flour hands and knead dough on a lightly floured surface. Shape into a smooth ball. Roll or pat to about ½-inch thickness and cut with a floured biscuit cutter or glass. Place the scones a little apart on a lightly greased baking sheet. Bake for about 10 minutes or until lightly golden. Split, butter, and serve hot for tea with marmalade or strawberry jam and whipped cream.

† LANCASTER TREACLE PARKIN

This ginger flavored cake should not be eaten until it has aged at least 2 weeks in an airtight container. It will keep for weeks and is ready to serve the unexpected guest for tea.

6 tbsp butter or margarine	½ cup light brown sugar
1 cup all-purpose flour	½ tsp nutmeg
2 cups Irish or Scotch oatmeal	1 cup golden syrup
½ cup candied fruit peel	½ tsp baking soda
2 tsp ground ginger	1 tbsp milk

Mix the shortening and flour with a single electric beater or with your hands. Add the oatmeal, candied fruit, ginger, sugar, and nutmeg and mix well. Warm the syrup just to lukewarm and mix with the baking soda dissolved in milk. Combine with other ingredients and when well mixed, place in a greased rectangular pan (8" x 12"). Bake one hour at 350° F. Cut into squares while still warm.

† *ENGLISH LOAF CAKE*

¾ cup sugar
4 tbsp butter
3 eggs
2 cups all-purpose flour
2 tsp baking powder
½ tsp salt

1 cup seedless raisins
1 tbsp orange peel
1 tbsp lemon peel
milk

Preheat the oven to 325° F. Cream the butter and sugar together until soft and fluffy. Beat in the eggs one by one. Combine the dry ingredients and add them, stirring until just blended. Add the raisins and the fruit peel cut very fine. Moisten with just enough milk to make the batter moist, but stiff enough so that the raisins won't sink. Place in a buttered loaf tin. Bake 1 hour.

† *LEMON SPONGE ROLL*

4 eggs
1 cup sugar
1 tsp lemon juice
1 tsp vanilla
1 cup sifted cake flour
⅛ tsp salt
confectioners' sugar

Filling
4 tbsp butter
3 eggs
1 egg yolk
1½ cups sugar
3 lemons
2 tbsp Cointreau

Line a large (10″ x 14″) baking sheet with heavy wax paper and butter it well. Separate the egg whites from the yolks. Beat the whites until stiff. Still beating, gradually add ¼ cup sugar. Set aside. In another bowl beat the yolks until lemon colored and thick. Add the lemon juice and vanilla. Combine the rest of the sugar with the flour and salt and then add alternately with the egg whites to the egg yolks, folding them in carefully. Preheat the oven to 400° F.

Spread the batter on the baking sheet, smoothing it evenly with a spatula. Bake 10 to 12 minutes, or until firm to the touch. Do not overbake. Turn out on a dampened dish towel liberally sprinkled with confectioners sugar. Cut off the edges quickly with a long, sharp knife or kitchen scissors, and tear away the wax paper. Roll up the cake along with the towel. Cool completely.

FILLING: Heat the butter in the top of a double boiler. Beat the eggs and egg yolk until light and add them with the sugar, the juice and grated rind of the lemons. Cook over boiling water, stirring constantly, until thick. Remove from the heat. Add the Cointreau and cool.

Unroll the cake and spread thickly with the filling. Reroll it (without the dish towel), and place the roll seam side down on a dessert platter. Sprinkle with confectioners' sugar.

† SEED CAKE

5 eggs	1½ tsp caraway seeds
1¼ cups sugar	⅓ cup candied lemon peel
½ lb butter	1 tsp vanilla
¼ tsp nutmeg	2 tbsp Cognac
2¾ cups sifted cake flour	

Preheat the oven to 350° F. Separate the eggs and beat the whites until stiff. Beat in ¼ cup of the sugar. Using another bowl but the same beater, beat the butter and the remaining sugar until light and creamy. Add the egg yolks one at a time, beating continuously. Add the remaining ingredients and mix until blended. Fold in the beaten whites and put in a buttered loaf tin. Sprinkle the top with sugar and a few caraway seeds, and bake for 1 hour.

† CORNISH SAFFRON BREAD

¼ tsp powdered saffron ½ cup lukewarm water
1 tsp salt 2¼ cups all-purpose flour
1 cup boiling water 1 cup currants
2 tbsp sugar ½ cup candied fruits, chopped
2 packages dry yeast

Combine the saffron, salt, boiling water, and sugar in a bowl and cool to lukewarm. Add the yeast dissolved in the lukewarm water. Stir in the flour, currants, and candied fruit. The mixture will be very moist. Cover and let rise until doubled in volume. Stir down, and let rise again. Stir down again and place in 2 small, buttered loaf tins. Cover and let rise again. Preheat the oven to 375° F, and bake 30 minutes. When cool, slice and spread the slices with fresh butter.

† SCOTCH SHORTBREAD

½ lb unsalted butter ¼ tsp baking powder
½ cup sugar ¼ tsp salt
¾ cup all-purpose flour ⅛ tsp almond extract
¼ cup rice flour

Preheat the oven to 350° F. Beat the butter and sugar together until light and creamy. Add the remaining ingredients, mixing until just blended. Roll out the mixture into a square ½ inch thick. Cut into small squares, about 1½ inches on a side. Place them on an ungreased baking sheet, pinching the corners and pressing down the sides gently. Bake 25 to 30 minutes.

SIX

The Admirable Eccentric

They all knew that they were funny, they even knew that
they were peculiar and rather gloried in it. . . .

NGAIO MARSH, *Death of a Peer*

In order to justify his position at the top of the heap, Lord Bumbershoot, host of the house party, should have better and special
qualifications. He should be the number one figure at the tea
table; dominate the scene. He isn't, and he doesn't. Apart from
the fact that the hostess, his wife, controls the teapot, the host is
guaranteed English drab. He is pale and as likely to be myopic
behind his monocle as the foolish-seeming aristocratic detective.
Only, in Lord Bumbershoot's case, it isn't a clever guise for a
penetrating brain. He really is simple. This leaves him prey to
the usual problem of the aristocrat: paralyzing awe of his man,
who is as intelligent and competent as he is not.

The sensible English gentleman has little sympathy for pol-
itics, less with religion, and none for people who are right. He
has an equal dislike of sobriety and punctuality, which he considers depressing virtues, and frightfully tiring. If given a choice,

he is hard put to decide which he dislikes more, "powerful per-
sonalities or earnest politicians," and is liable to prefer "the
cheerful inefficient," as Lord Caterham does in Agatha Christie's *The Seven Dials Mystery,* even if there's a chance he's the
murderer. The gentleman's sense of sportsmanship is so highly
developed that cheating at cards is infinitely more reprehensible
to him than murder or adultery; the *crime passionel* is almost
wholly unknown in England. His idea of excitement is to read
catalogues of forthcoming sales of rare editions (just as his
lady's is to read seed catalogues). The English gentleman could
fade through a wall, leaving nothing behind but a bristling
mustache and a pile of newspapers.

With the awe-inspiring English mastery of minimal language, Lord Bumbershoot goes through an entire lifetime on
grunts, snorts, embarrassed throat clearings, startled coughs of
amusement and, at his most articulate, is driven to comment,
"Oh, I say!" It will be a difficult situation that elicits that much:
his daughter has elected to marry an American and/or the detective. A murder has interfered with the shooting season. Friends
have stopped asking him and his wife to dinner because they
suspect him of murder. After such a major outpouring, it will be
necessary to conduct his next twenty years of communication by
rustling the pages of his newspaper vehemently, when angered,
or stirring his tea with a lolloping stroke, if pleased.

When not being hospitable over tea or whisky-and-soda,
the English gentleman's principal occupation is seeing to the
property. The aristocrat is, above all, agrarian man. His animals,
his woods, his streams, his meadows are of primary concern.
Whenever the author wishes to get rid of the squire for a stretch
of time, she sends him off with a stick, a dog or two, and his
steward to see his farms. If he heads for the woods, she adds a
cap, his shotgun, and his gamekeeper instead of the steward.
Nothing soothes him so quickly, in times of trouble or after the
effort of thinking, as a walk to see the pigs.

So truly is the Englishman a man of property, a murderer is

a good deal easier to condone ("After all, the fella was bottled, wa'nt he?") than a poacher. Ah, that makes the blood rise. Should the squire see something moving in the trees, he takes a potshot at it on the supposition that anything that moves in the woods *should* be shot. If it's not an animal, it surely is a poacher. Hanging is too delicate. Steal my daughter first.

The English gentleman does not, however, let his love of property show. His home is his castle, but it is in studied disrepair. He will let the marble balustrade fall, the silk drapes fade, the old place fall into a shambles, or affect it—if he hasn't managed the real thing by feverishly poor investments—and feel the better for it. Aristocrats are vague as anything about money. They like losing it, to prove how little they care. (Money is grubby, that's a known fact.) No stone is too small to turn in rejection of ostentation, a tendency given support by lingering traces of puritanism. However, when an English gentleman has his man break in his tweeds and boots for him, it has nothing to do with self-denial. It is done simply as witness to the fact that all he possesses—title, money, property—comes from way back. We may, and he would like us to, assume that his hacking jacket was originally worn at the Battle of Hastings by Ethelred the Unready, a great-uncle twice removed, don't y'know. A house that shows its age is just one more method of showing how above it all he is, and just how close in lineage he comes to the divine right of kings. Every other vagary is directly descended from this.

The scope of eccentricity for the gentleman is broad enough to encompass everything from tottering domicile on ill-managed grounds preyed on by staff and itinerant poachers to personal idiosyncrasies. No Englishman worth his breeding fails in eccentricity. It is required. It is expected. It is desirable. It is cultivated and polished, preened over pleasurably; if it were not, it could be taken for lunacy, which is common, and confined, mercifully, to the lower classes. The very awareness of the effect one is making is what separates the eccentric from the madman.

Eccentricity is freedom; madness, the opposite. Eccentricity is freedom from convention and conformity, from toeing the mark or needing to, from dependence on good will or good opinion. This freedom to be one's self is the greatest luxury of the upper class.

Eccentricity has probably shorted more class rebellions than we will ever know. Why get riled up about privilege when you can patronize a peer? A good laugh at the local over Lord Bumbershoot is as good as a rise. A chuckle at a marchioness is like a chicken in the pot.

SEVEN

The Gardener:
Plots and Plants

Lady Coote . . . nerved herself to speak to MacDonald, the
head gardener, who was surveying the domain over which
he ruled with an autocratic eye. MacDonald was a very
chief and prince among head gardeners. He knew his place
—which was to rule. And he ruled—despotically.

AGATHA CHRISTIE, *The Seven Dials Mystery*

Gardeners are more important in mysteries for what they rule
over: gardening sheds, endhouses, conservatories, and late
grapes; what they are in possession of: flowerpots to put over
footprints, tins of arsenic, and information about the condition
of the flower beds before and after the crime, than for any direct
contribution they make.

In classic footprint cases, for example, they are referred to
obliquely, as in: "Jones just laid in that bed of campion this
morning *after* the rain." Or, "Thank Heaven, Reginald's gardener ain't one of those conscientious blighters who can't let a

cactus alone even in winter, or he would have lifted these, and spoiled the mark of the suitcase imbedded behind the pots." Or, "Boggs says the third branch of the rose tree was definitely not snapped before tea yesterday afternoon." The snapping of rose twigs, sensed from afar in the soul of the gardener, can establish the time of the murder far more accurately than rigor. To the flower-nanny eyes of the gardener, cooing over every leaf, and refusing to plant what anybody wants, the jostling of a rose head is noted, and the plundering of a poppy will send him running, cap in hand, into the breakfast room.

The same observations about the conditions of her plots and plants can, of course, be made by Her Ladyship. Her Ladyship goes to sleep at night with the exact slant of her prize larkspurs or night-scented stock imprinted on her brain, much as an architect might recall the geometric incline of a hill, or a general his troop deployment (the Englishwoman fights her battles through her garden).

Not only are gardeners taciturn, and up with the birds, they are persons of temperament. They are given to flying off the trowel at Her Ladyship for interference and, subsequently, skulking in the kitchen garden, rattling the arsenic tin in a meaningful manner, or giving notice at a moment when it gives an impression of implication in the crime. But unless he is young, and bears a striking resemblance to His Lordship, the gardener is not often guilty, whatever his temperament.

Gardens in mysteries, based on the English pattern, are a mixed seed packet. Great beds lie waiting for the murderer's footprints, for the Horsy Lady to weed or gather opulent bouquets for the church chancel, for Her Ladyship to quarrel with the gardener about, for after-dinner strollers to be overlooked in. The garden will have foxgloves (handy for fatal doses of digitalis), delphiniums; tall, spiky, rambling things. All one needs to do to have a good garden is to trench the sweet peas, talk about bulbs, argue knowledgeably about whether fishheads or bonemeal make a better mulch for roses, and war with the gardener.

Ignorance of gardening, like dialects used to detect the enemy during war, can be a trap. Anyone who goes into a rockery, ostensibly to weed, and comes up with a campanula may be subject to immediate arrest. Clearly, an imposter.

The well-stocked garden has a wide selection of poisons, supposedly for spraying bugs, handily available in the dilapidated toolshed with instructions for use, neatly posted. The considerate hostess goes one step further, and has individual packets already made up for her guests to mix in each other's coffee after luncheon in place of sugar (less fattening).

Flowers are banked against the house where more rain-muddied beds wait impatiently for the telltale imprint of the murderer's foot, as he makes a soft landing from the ivy. Guessing this, the clever murderer has put his shoes on backward or squeezed into a pair that are too small for him. This game of footsie is not, as a rule, successful. The detectives are there ahead of him. They can tell heights, weights, and the true direction the foot was heading from the depth and angle of the print.

There is no sense in having a murder without a healthy stand of rhododendron, and no sense having a gardener other than to fight with Her Ladyship about them. Keeps everyone, including the rhododendron, in trim.

One of the advantages of rhododendrons is that they keep their leaves all winter. In fact, in winter they look about as good as they ever do. Quite unaccountably, of course, rhododendron can go into bloom, and splash color lavishly about. The sensitive murderer will avoid that season in favor of something more ominous.

Rhododendrons grow to heights of about thirty feet, and have dark, shiny leaves like spindly elephants' ears. As their branches are also rather spindly, and branch high up, they provide a sufficiently dense shield, yet serve nicely for lurking, if that is desired. Lurking is done, first, by the murderer, to pick his moment (usually, when the butler closes the drapes, and turns down the lights). After the murder, there will be more people in the garden than in the house, and no one in bed, except the victim. Then, the lurking is taken over by all the amateur detectives among the guests, spying out the movements of whomever they suspect.

A really nice house will have both formal and kitchen gardens. Kitchen gardens can serve such useful purposes as providing strange little eggheaded detectives with outsize marrows to toss over the wall and bean a murderer with. A small formal garden can serve as an arena for a murder. Heavy shrubs of strong-needled holly become walls surrounding flowers and stone benches. Quick-footed guests, responding to shouts and screams, can cut off the only exits for the murderer. Actually, the victim will turn out to have been shot from a mole hole, or an aged apple tree, or to have died of spontaneous combustion, even if a dangerously handsome woman is found standing directly over him with a smoking revolver.

All gardens must have flagstone paths for evening strolls. Wherever the English are, they walk. They put on their brogues, and they walk. They put on their country shoes, and they walk. They put on their oxfords, and they walk. The shoes are brown, have thick soles, lace up or buckle, are made of wonderful leather and, like all English clothes, are made to last.

After-dinner strolls are an essential part of the English character. With the fidelity of cuckoos emerging from their clocks, the English bestir themselves. If a catastrophe has shattered everything but the drawing room, they step through the French windows, parasols up to fend off the flying debris, and set off over the rubble.

In foreign climes, riots or plagues would not stop the same performance. It is a necessary part of digestion, and a preface to sleep. It is as curative of disturbed physical or mental tone as tea to the soul, or a trip to the Colonies for a broken heart. Who knows what would happen to the food or their dreams without a walk? In war zones or earthquakes, they may become targets or fall in fissures, but they walk.

At home, if not walking in the garden, the English take to the footpaths. The countryside is latticed with public footpaths, which cause people to pop up like rabbits in a shooting gallery in other people's gardens. People are constantly stepping over stiles, and setting off.

The stroll occupies almost as important a place in the health regime of an Englishman as windows thrown open to ensure gales of fresh air blowing into the bedroom at night. No self-respecting English home is warmer than 65 degrees and, if the windows are closed, the family is clearly out of the country, or has suffered a loss or humiliation that requires that they attempt to suffocate themselves. During the after-dinner stroll in the garden something will be overheard or seen that lights flames of jealousy, or otherwise ignites the eavesdropper. The overheard conversation should run, in part: "You shall be sorry for this." Known voice, to be suspected later, to unknown listener.

The evening stroll, when enjoyed by two gentlemen no longer young, may take on the philosophical overtones of which the English are masters: "After all, people have to behave themselves, swallow their feelings and that sort of thing." And, of course, if they only would there would be no murders.

EIGHT

The Flighty Daughter: How Debs are Bred

She had a supremely natural manner and, as she looked up smiling, the faint wild rose flush deepened in her cheeks. Her eyes were a very dark blue—like cornflowers.

AGATHA CHRISTIE, *The Seven Dials Mystery*

Nice girls wake in the morning with sunlight on their counterpanes. At night they fall asleep in pyjamas before their bedroom fires. The windows of their bedrooms float in white organdie curtains sprigged with currant blossoms, and birds sing outside. They have fair hair, cheeks inclined to blush like wild roses, cornflower blue eyes, and two black spaniels. Nice girls have French maids who pack them up for house parties. Their fathers dote on them; they behave in a dutiful fashion toward their mothers; and come out, with flurry and fanfare and a tent on the lawn, at eighteen. They have cupboards full of frocks: black georgette for dreary occasions, petunia crepe and muslin frills, picked up at Worth, for afternoon teas and dancing. Beneath them, debs wear shockingly little, and what there is is crepe de Chine.

There is more than a bit of the devil in a Flighty Daughter. To the horror of a maiden aunt, she may have bobbed her hair. When taken out by a beau, she has oysters; when she wants information about the staff, she has rich cocoa with the housekeeper; when angered, stamps her foot. She often occasions house parties, having asked a number of her friends, plus an assortment of spotty louts and tiny Tims to bulk out the group, for the weekend. They will play jazz on the gramophone and dance in the library, or play the wireless and dance in the Big Hall, and do other flaming youth things.

A Flighty Daughter is as inclined as anyone to come through French doors, but when she does, she drifts. She drifts as much as the three-day snows, so essential to tying up a mystery. There is, altogether, a fairly insubstantial quality about her. She kisses the air beside one's cheek or, if too far away for even that, blows a kiss and hopes it lands. It is doubtful that she eats on the same formidable scale as other participants in mysteries, as she is stylishly thin. For all her slimness, however, she is as strong as a whipcord. When she drinks, as scandalously she does, she has a pink gin among the potted palms on an afternoon up for shopping in London. If she's really flighty, and heading for deep trouble, she has gin and vermouth. When she goes off to tennis parties, she speeds away in her little two-seater. Running up to London, she takes the family Hispano, which she drives at daring speeds. There's just no holding her down.

Debs are fair game for Latin gigolos. When a deb goes to a watering hole, she must be closely watched by her old dragon of a nanny, or she will become involved with a dance instructor quicker than you can clack a castanet. Almost as dangerous is the tennis instructor, flicking his racquet in a devastating manner, for though he is English he is a thoroughly bad hat. And frightfully charming, naturally. One of those younger sons destined to go rotten, live by their wits, and that sort of thing. Too handsome or too athletic men with too many white teeth never turn out well. They are invariably weak—a characteristic worth remembering when going over a suspect list. All is for naught, if the deb falls in love with someone who is "not quite the thing." She must, then, be packed off to some penal colony like the States to forget. Meanwhile, the family will pay off the beggar, and substitute someone more suitable (with monocle and a job in the City) to meet her at the boat on her return.

Debs past their first youth are inclined to be called by the same nicknames they had as children, so that when they go to Old School reunions, someone can hail them across the quad as "Bunch," "Bundle," or "Socks," and still get a response. As they rush across the green, bells ring, nostalgia hits, and the cooks in the senior hall stir up a mess of potage—the same mess of potage they were stirring up in their wonderful old trad way when the deb was at school. Maybe a little more salt.

The education of a deb is costly, but simple. She must be able to arrange flowers, pour tea, laugh musically on any and all occasions, and balance her dress allowance. Any other skills, however pleasant, are wholly superfluous and some, like intelligence, definitely get in the way. Unlike their silly-seeming brothers, aristocratic little girls never do outgrow their silliness to become shining lights of society.

After she comes out, should the deb be orphaned, made penniless by an automobile accident or an airplane crash, she will find herself the object of wintry smiles from former acquaintances. One simply does not raise one's head after a fall from substance. But it may be worth it. Orphaned, she is in line for a major role in a mystery, and a whack at the detective or some hobbledehoy of a newspaper reporter, who will scoop her up in newsprint and carry her off to a little white cot in Devon, where she can forget the silverplate (and Old Dodders hanging in his pantry), and raise masses of little hobbledehoys amidst pink and purple hollyhocks.

NINE

Fatal Feeds: The Scene Is Set

Nothing goes so well with a hot fire and buttered crumpets as a wet day without and a good dose of comfortable horrors within. The heavier the lashing of the rain and the ghastlier the details, the better the flavour seems to be.

DOROTHY L. SAYERS, *Strong Poison*

A country house must obviously have a Great Hall. Though in periods of calm Christmas pantomimes or charades are acted out there, in murderous days it is used to gather the members of a small house party together before the fire; to announce the master's demise to the staff; and later, for a spellbinding recapitulation of the crime by a saturnine detective.

The snowstorm, the worst in years, falls only after the

guests are safely tucked in. Murderers have a meteorologist's instinct for unusual weather conditions. Should nature's arts still be deemed insufficient, the murderer will cut the wires of the one telephone in the downstairs hall. This frees him for occupations other than eavesdropping, which is time-consuming and, for such an active person, boring. Once the guests are secured, no mail will arrive, no newspapers come. Winter is absolutely recommended for murder. It confines the arena to the indoors, and saves on search parties. It is thanks only to the general mildness of English winters that anyone is alive there today.

Outside, nature does more than lighten or darken the mood. It demands an active role. Wind howls at the door of mysteries. Rattles the shutters. Knocks twigs against the windows. Rumbles, ominous as an oracle, in a thunderous sky. Nature furnishes the three-day snow that makes the road impassable, cuts off the house party from the outside world, prevents them from calling in the police, and plays into the killer's hands. It also supplies the rain that makes the flower beds receptive to the footsteps of the murderer.

If nature is calm, jealousy rumbles. The guests are prepared to supply their own heat and light. There is a femme fatale in the crowd. This means there will be much dueling with the eyes, and mocking laughter launched through a scarlet slash of a mouth.

Femme fatales are a nasty piece of work. Most of them are past their first youth (they are thirty-five); hard, cold beauties who spend as much time before their mirrors as Snow White's stepmother, to whom they bear a striking resemblance, complete with startlingly white skin and brilliant black hair. They have long nails polished, appropriately, in red. They are impossibly cruel to their impossibly ugly and/or old husbands, snap other men like twigs, tease their loyal retainers, but are inclined occasionally to be darling and witty to their friends of whom they have, unaccountably, vast numbers. They wear Lelong models that are a shaft of silver shot with flame; the odor of Chypre wafts from their furs as they settle into their Rolls, and they have eau-de-Nil drawing rooms.

To make sure she is not-quite-nice, the femme fatale is frequently an actress. Nothing strikes fire or ice into the heart of an Englishman faster than the glamorous actress. The number of actresses who have fallen in mysteries is well and away beyond statistical possibility. If they are not themselves victim or murderess, the burning passions they inspire cause the crime. "And all goes down before them."

No one remotely involved with the stage has real feelings. Fame is the god and publicity, its means of worship. Any show of authentic feeling is brought out as a rarity worth remarking. If a femme fatale appears only harmlessly vain and shallow, she will prove to have a streak of mania a yard wide that, much to the consternation of her husband and friends, will cause her to crack out in a vendetta of some sort laying waste around her in fabulous fashion. Should her mirror tell her she's getting old and wrinkly (she is thirty-six), it will have the effect of a starting gun at a dog race. She will whip out the poison jars as if they were cold cream, and slather them on the next person who comments on a wrinkle. Hell hath no fury like endangered narcissism.

Meanwhile, seething in the wings, is a vivid case of repression: someone's wife, the Drab Dame. Drab Dames are dumpy and have always gotten the short end of the stick. Reverse Cinderellas, they are eaten up with envy of their fairer sisters. A drab woman always wears the wrong clothes, lets her hair scraggle, and timidly says the wrong things, which absolutely set her handsome husband on the edge of his chair. If she wears a hat, she will tilt it over the eye if it's meant to be worn on the back of the head, and wear it on the back of the head if it's meant to be tilted over the eye. She has no clothes sense. And she's tired of knowing it. So tired she could kill somebody. Invariably, she does.

But the weak, handsome man among the guests will be suspected. The weak, bad-but-not-dreadful man is easily recognized. He mixes himself a pink gin, keeps himself beautifully groomed, gambles, and has a tortoiseshell toilet set. Good grooming, good looks, with religious feeling and emotion, are just a few more things that make an Englishman wary. The weak, handsome man has either had money and gone through it, or thinks he should have. He may have done a little prospecting for gold in South America or Big-Game Hunting in Africa, uses his oversupply of charm to advantage with the ladies, and is not above swindling and lying. But he hasn't the panache for murder. He couldn't do anything as active and positive as murder. He'd rather cadge the odd fiver. Murderers come off rather better than suspects. They have panache.

To cool rampant passions, the Great Hall is drafty. Great houses are as liable to have drafts as their guests are to be poisoned. Owners of Great Houses believe in tradition, not central heating. If murderers were a little more patient, their victims might succumb to a chill. These Spartan conditions affect the construction of the rooms, and the amount of food and drink consumed. The more lustily one eats, the warmer he stays. It does not affect the dressing; women continue to show their long, lovely arms and bare backs. As the biggest rooms are the draftiest of all, they have enormous fireplaces. This is, however, advantageous. Fireplaces are superb dramatic focal points. And one needs all the grates he can get for burning evidence.

Around the fireplace they huddle; the women in their inadequate chiffons; the men, with glass in hand—leaning against the mantel, a polished pump poised on the fender—or sunk comfortably in leather armchairs. The group is small, so that we may know them better, and limited to what we know and like, or don't know and detest. There are bounders who make us irritable, charmers to make us nervous, and pretty, fair-haired ladies to protect. Outside, it grows dark. Drapes are drawn against the night. The fire crackles, casting strange shadows on the walls, deepening the darkness, while anticipation builds like an appetite for dinner. The light of the fire touches the prisms of the chandelier as it flickers; it shines ominously through a decanter of port.

The guests are ready. Murder is served.

† FATAL FEEDS

Fatal feeds are those marvelous leftovers from the opulent Victorian days before, as Nancy Mitford says in *Love in a Cold Climate,* "The age of luxury was ended and that of comfort had begun." This type of meal survives, if somewhat diminished, on Sundays and holidays. At a house party it behooves the guests to be none too dainty, when it is served. This may be the last meal for a long time they'll enjoy, or, simply, the last.

FATAL FEEDS
(for eight people)
   Melons Oporto
   Chicken Liver Pâté
   Cold Tomato and Orange Soup
   Mackerel in Gooseberry Sauce
   Sole Mornay
   Chicken Casserole
   Roast Goose with Sausage and Chestnut Dressing
   Roast Pheasant with Bread Sauce
   Boiled Bacon with Parsley Sauce

Roast Lamb with Onion Sauce
Roast Pork Ménagère
Standing Rib Roast of Beef with Yorkshire Pudding
Lancashire Hot Pot
Braised Veal with Vegetables
Venison Steaks with Cumberland Sauce
Leeks Vinaigrette
Baked Fennel
Broccoli en Purée
Cabbage in Cream
New Potatoes in Herb Butter
Macédoine of Vegetables
Peas in Heavy Cream
Jerusalem Artichoke Chips
Boodle's Orange Fool
Peach Flan
Plum Pudding
Royal English Trifle
Scotch Woodcock

† *MELONS OPORTO*

4 canteloupes   1 pint port
½ cup sugar

Cut the canteloupes in half. Remove the seeds and fibers, and cut a little slice off the bottom of each so that the fruit will sit well on the plates. Sprinkle each with 1 tbsp sugar and put ¼ cup of port in each half. Cover and chill thoroughly before serving. This is a good beginning or end of any meal.

† CHICKEN LIVER PÂTÉ

1 lb chicken livers	2 tsp salt
4 tbsp butter	1 tsp white pepper
4 shallots, minced	½ cup chicken bouillon
2 tbsp chopped parsley	2 tbsp brandy
½ tsp allspice	½ cup heavy cream
½ tsp marjoram	½ cup chopped pistachio nuts (optional)

Trim the livers and cut them in pieces. Heat the butter and sauté the shallots and livers for 3 to 4 minutes, stirring frequently. Remove from the pan with a slotted spoon, cool, and put in a blender. If you do not have a blender, mash the livers to a fine paste. Add the parsley, the spices, and the liquids and blend to a purée. If you wish, you may stir in the pistachio nuts, but do not blend them. Put the purée in a buttered mold. Cover and refrigerate for 24 hours before unmolding and serving with French bread or buttered toast.

† COLD TOMATO AND ORANGE SOUP

5 cups vegetable-tomato juice	1 quart chicken broth
1 bay leaf	2 oranges
1 tsp sugar	½ lemon
6 tbsp butter	1 cup heavy cream
5 tbsp flour	1 tbsp chopped parsley

Simmer the juice, bay leaf, and sugar for half an hour over very low heat. Heat the butter in a large saucepan over medium heat and blend in the flour, cooking and stirring for 2 minutes. Do not let the mixture brown. Add 1 cup of chicken broth and stir until smooth. Add the rest of the broth and the strained tomato juice. Bring to a boil and simmer 20 minutes.

Shred the outer rind of the oranges coarsely and boil 1 minute. Drain and freshen with cold water. Squeeze the juice from the oranges and lemon. The combined juices should measure about ⅔ of a cup. Remove the soup from the heat, add the juice and most of the shredded rind. Cool and add the cream. Chill in the refrigerator for 2 to 3 hours. Serve very cold in bouillon cups garnished with a little of the orange rind and chopped parsley.

† MACKEREL IN GOOSEBERRY SAUCE

8 small mackerel	½ cup gooseberry preserve
salt and pepper	½ cup heavy cream
flour	2 tsp lemon juice
4 tbsp butter	½ tsp salt

Fillet the mackerel, which should be very fresh. Season the fillets with salt and pepper and dip lightly in flour. Heat the butter in a large skillet, and when very hot, fry the fillets until brown on both sides. Transfer to a heated platter and serve with the previously prepared sauce.

GOOSEBERRY SAUCE: Combine the gooseberry preserves with the cream, and heat in a double boiler. Just before serving, add the lemon juice and salt.

† SOLE MORNAY

8 sole fillets	1 cup fish stock
½ tsp salt	1 cup rich milk
1 cup dry white wine	2 egg yolks, lightly beaten
water	1 cup grated Gruyère or mild
1 small onion, sliced	Cheddar cheese
4 tbsp butter	1 cup cream
6 tbsp flour	white pepper

Place the fillets in a large skillet or electric frying pan. Sprinkle with salt. Add the white wine and enough water to just cover. Add the sliced onion. Simmer very gently until the fish flakes when a fork is inserted. Remove the fillets very carefully with a wide slotted spatula and place them in a heatproof platter, spacing them so that they can be easily served. Keep warm. Turn up the heat under the water and boil down the liquid with any trimmings (skin or bones) that you may have been able to get from your fish dealer. When the liquid measures approximately 1 cup, strain it into a measuring cup.

Preheat the broiler.

Heat the butter in a saucepan and stir in the flour. Cook for about 2 minutes without letting the mixture brown. Add the fish stock and the milk and stir until smooth and thick. Add the beaten egg yolks and stir for another minute. Remove from the heat and stir in the cheese and finally the cream. Taste for seasoning, adding salt and pepper to taste. Pour the sauce over the fish and brown lightly under the broiler.

Serve with boiled potatoes and garnish with sprigs of parsley.

† CHICKEN CASSEROLE

8 chicken quarters	1 cup dry white wine
¼ lb salt pork	2 cups chicken bouillon
1 lb mushrooms	salt and pepper
4 tbsp butter	1 tbsp butter, mixed with
16 small onions, peeled	1½ tbsp flour
16 tiny carrots	½ lemon
	chopped parsley

Wash and wipe the chicken pieces. Wash the salt pork in warm water to remove excess salt, and cut in small dice. Trim, wash and dry the mushrooms and chop coarsely.

Heat 2 tbsp butter in a large skillet. Sauté the pork and mushrooms for 5 minutes, stirring frequently. Transfer them to a deep casserole. In the same skillet brown the chicken quarters, adding more butter when necessary. Place them in the casserole. Finally sauté the onions and carrots briefly in the same skillet, and set aside.

Preheat the oven to 325° F.

Pour the wine into the skillet and scrape all the juices adhering to the pan. Add the bouillon and bring to a boil. Strain the liquid into the casserole, season with salt and pepper, and bake for 1 hour, adding the vegetables for the last 30 minutes of cooking.

Place the chicken on a heated platter and surround with the onions and carrots. Quickly boil down the liquid in the casserole by half, adding the flour and butter paste bit by bit and whisking until smooth. Taste for seasoning, adding the juice of ½ lemon. Pour a little of the sauce over the chicken, saving the rest to serve in a sauce boat. Sprinkle with chopped parsley, serve with sautéed diced potatoes.

† ROAST GOOSE WITH SAUSAGE AND CHESTNUT DRESSING

10-lb goose	½ lb sausage meat
1 lb chestnuts	1 tbsp chopped parsley
3 tbsp butter	½ tsp sage
½ cup chopped onion	1½ cups fresh bread crumbs
	salt and pepper

Place the heart, neck, gizzard, and wing tips of the goose in a pan of water with a slice of onion, some celery leaves, and 1 tsp salt. Bring to a boil covered. Simmer 2½ hours. This stock will be used for the gravy.

Cut a cross on the flat side of each chestnut. Place chestnuts in a pan of cold water and bring to a boil. Boil 1 minute and move the pan to the side of the heat so that the water will stay hot without boiling. Take out the nuts one at a time and remove the outer and inner skin. Boil the shelled chestnuts 20 minutes or until tender. Chop ½ cup of the nuts coarsely and purée the rest in a blender with a little boiling water or force them through a food mill into a large bowl.

Heat the butter in a saucepan and cook the onions until soft without browning. Stir in the sausage meat and brown well. Add the mixture to the puréed chestnuts along with the chopped chestnuts, the parsley, sage, and bread crumbs. Mix thoroughly and season to taste.

Preheat the oven to 450° F. Pack the cavity of the goose loosely with the dressing. Lace the opening with small skewers and kitchen twine, and bind the wings and legs to the body with skewers or twine. Prick the skin all over with a fork. Wipe the bird well with a towel and rub with salt. Place in a roasting pan on a rack breast side up.

Roast the goose 20 minutes at the high temperature. Reduce the heat quickly to 350° by opening the oven door. Turn the goose on its side, remove any fat from the pan, and baste with a little boiling water using a syringe baster. Repeat the fat removal and basting process several times during the cooking. Roast 2½ hours, turning it on the other side halfway through the cooking.

Transfer the goose to a large platter. Remove the fat from the pan and strain 2 cups of the goose stock into the roasting pan. Bring to a boil, scraping the juices adhering to the pan. Stir in 2 tbsp butter and strain into a sauce boat. Garnish the goose with watercress, and for special occasions drape a garland of pan-broiled link sausages over the breast.

Serve with small, boiled Brussels sprouts and baked acorn squash.

† ROAST PHEASANT WITH BREAD SAUCE

Allow 1 pheasant (2½ to 3 lbs) for 2 servings. Wipe the birds and sprinkle them inside and out with salt and pepper. Tie the legs together and skewer them to the body. Place them on a rack in a roasting pan, and cover the breasts with bacon cut ⅛ inch thick. Roast at 350° F for 2¼ to 2½ hours depending on the size. Baste occasionally with melted butter. Serve them on a platter and garnish with watercress. Accompany them with red currant jelly and freshly made bread sauce.

† BREAD SAUCE

2 cups milk	½ tsp salt
1 onion, sliced thick	⅛ tsp pepper
3 cloves	½ cup soft white bread crumbs
½ bay leaf	2 tbsp butter
⅛ tsp thyme	2 tbsp cream

Heat the milk over moderate heat with the onion, cloves, herbs, salt, and pepper for 15 minutes. Strain into another saucepan. Just before serving add the bread crumbs and simmer 2 to 3 minutes, stirring until the sauce is smooth and thick. Stir in the butter and cream. Heat but do not boil.

† BOILED BACON WITH PARSLEY SAUCE

2 lb daisy ham	PARSLEY SAUCE
2 cups white wine	3 tbsp butter
1 bay leaf	3 tbsp flour
pinch of thyme	⅔ cup milk
1 onion stuck with a clove	1 cup cooking liquid
1 carrot cut in chunks	2 tbsp chopped parsley
6 peppercorns	1 tsp salt
	¼ tsp white pepper

Place the ham in a kettle with the wine, herbs, vegetables, and peppercorns. Add enough water to cover the meat. Bring to a boil and simmer 30 minutes per lb. Serve in a deep platter with the parsley sauce poured over it, and surround with boiled potatoes.

PARSLEY SAUCE: Heat the butter and stir in the flour, cooking for 2 minutes over low heat, but do not let the butter brown. Add the milk and cooking liquid, and stir until thick and smooth. Add the parsley, salt, and pepper.

† ROAST LAMB WITH ONION SAUCE

6 lb leg of lamb	5 peppercorns
salt and pepper	1½ cups chopped onions
ONION SAUCE	3 tbsp butter
1½ cups milk	3 tbsp flour
pinch of mace	2 tbsp cream
½ tsp salt	

Order the leg either boned and rolled or with the bone left in. Trim off any excess fat. Preheat oven to 325° F. Rub the meat with salt and pepper. Place in a roasting pan and roast 12 minutes per lb for rare lamb (140° F on a roasting thermometer) and 20 minutes per lb for well done (175°-180°). When done let it stand outside the oven while you are making the sauce.

ONION SAUCE: Simmer the milk with the seasonings and onions until the onions are soft. In a separate saucepan heat the butter and stir in the flour, cooking 2 minutes without browning. Strain the milk from the onions into the mixture and stir until thick and smooth. Add the cream. Remove the peppercorns from the onions. Force the onions through a food mill or purée them in a blender. Add them to the sauce and season well with salt and pepper.

Place the roast on a serving platter. Pour off the fat from the pan. Add ½ cup boiling water and scrape the juices adhering to the pan. Add more water as desired. Season with salt and pepper if necessary and strain into a gravy boat. Accompany the roast with the onion sauce, the pan gravy and mint or currant jelly.

† ROAST PORK MÉNAGÈRE

5 to 6 lb loin roast of pork	8 potatoes
salt and pepper	3 large onions, sliced
1 tsp rosemary	butter
	parsley

Preheat the oven to 350° F. Rub the roast with salt, pepper, and rosemary. Peel the potatoes and onions, and slice them ⅛ inch thick. Butter a roasting pan or heatproof casserole, and line with a layer of potatoes and then a layer of onion rings. Dot with butter and sprinkle with salt and pepper. Repeat the process until the vegetables are used up, ending with a layer of potato slices. Place the roast on top of the vegetables. Pour in just enough water to cover the potatoes. Bring the water to a boil on top of the stove, and then roast in the oven for 2½ to 3 hours, depending on the size of the roast.

Serve the roast on a platter surrounded with the vegetables. Sprinkle with freshly chopped parsley.

† STANDING RIB ROAST OF BEEF
WITH YORKSHIRE PUDDING

Order a 7 to 8 lb rib roast of the highest quality. Preheat the oven to 375° F. Heat the roasting pan, which has been greased with 2 tbsp vegetable shortening or beef drippings. Sprinkle the meat generously with salt and freshly ground black pepper. Insert a meat thermometer into the fleshy center of the roast, and roast at 16 minutes per lb for rare meat (140° when done), 18 to 20 minutes per lb for medium rare (160° when done). Allow 15 to 20 minutes for the roast to rest outside the oven to make for easier carving.

A boned rib roast, a rump roast, or a sirloin roast may be cooked the same way, but the meat should be placed on a rack in the pan and basted periodically. A beef tenderloin should be cooked at 400° F, allowing 15 minutes per lb, and should be basted frequently.

DISH GRAVY: Remove almost all the fat from the roasting pan. Add ½ cup of boiling water or bouillon and, if you like, 4 tbsp madeira. Scrape off all the juices adhering to the pan, stir, and cook until all is well blended. Add more liquid if you like. Season to taste and strain into a hot gravy boat.

THICK GRAVY: Remove all but about 4 tbsp fat in the pan. Scrape with a fork to loosen all juices adhering to the pan. Add 4 tbsp flour and stir into the fat until the mixture is brown and smooth. Add two cups of stock, bouillon, or water, stir over heat with the fork and let simmer for 5 minutes. Season with salt and pepper, and strain into a hot gravy boat.

† YORKSHIRE PUDDING

When you have put the roast in the oven, mix the following batter and let it stand at room temperature until time to bake, approximately 40 minutes before serving.

4 eggs	1¼ tsp salt
3 cups nonfat milk	4 tbsp beef drippings
2 cups flour	

Beat the eggs with 1 cup of milk until completely blended. Add the flour mixed with the salt and beat until smooth. Add the rest of the milk gradually, beating constantly. This should take 3 to 4 minutes. Spoon about 4 tbsp hot fat from the pan in which the meat is cooking and pour into a large rectangular, preheated pan, coating the bottom and sides well. Pour in the batter, which should be about ½ inch deep. Bake about 40 minutes in the oven with the roast, removing the roast when it is done for its resting period. Or if you are fortunate enough to have two ovens, bake at 425° F for 30 minutes. Cut in squares and serve either around the roast or on a separate platter. It is traditional to eat this with dish gravy.

† *LANCASHIRE HOT POT*

2 lbs boned shoulder of lamb	3 lamb kidneys
2 tbsp butter or margarine	¼ lb mushrooms
1 large onion, diced	12 oysters
2 tbsp flour	salt and pepper
1 cup canned bouillon	6 potatoes

Cut the lamb into slices ¾ inch thick. Brown slices in butter or margarine in a skillet and transfer them to a greased earthenware casserole. Sauté the onions in the same pan until soft. Add the flour and brown without scorching. Add the bouillon and stir until the gravy is thick. Season with salt and pepper. Set aside.

Remove the film and fatty core from the kidneys. Slice them and put the pieces on the meat. Trim, wash, and slice the mushrooms and lay them on the kidneys. Cover with the oysters and their liquor. Sprinkle with salt and pepper and pour in the gravy carefully.

Peel and slice the potatoes. Cover the oysters with layer of potatoes and top that with another layer decoratively arranged with the slices overlapping. Cover and bake for 2 hours at 300° F. Remove the cover and increase the heat to 375° F until the potatoes have browned. Serve directly from the pot.

† BRAISED VEAL WITH VEGETABLES

5 tbsp butter
2 stalks celery, diced
2 medium sized onions, chopped
1 clove garlic, minced
1 carrot, sliced

4 lb roast of veal, boned and rolled
2 tbsp salad oil
½ tsp rosemary
salt and pepper
2 cups canned bouillon
4 cups small potato balls
3 cups diced carrots
4 cups shelled peas
2 tbsp chopped parsley

Heat 3 tbsp butter in a skillet and cook the celery, onions, garlic, and carrot until soft. Transfer the vegetables to a deep casserole and spread over the bottom.

Preheat the oven to 350° F. In the same skillet heat remaining 2 tbsp butter and oil, and brown the veal on all sides. This will take about 15 minutes. Place the meat on the vegetables in the casserole, and sprinkle with the rosemary, salt, and pepper. Cover tightly. Cook in the oven 1 hour. Turn the veal over and add the bouillon. Braise 1 more hour.

Prepare and boil the vegetables separately in salted water, allowing 10 to 15 minutes, or until each is tender. Drain and season with butter, salt, and pepper, still keeping them separate. Arrange them in small mounds around the edge of a serving platter. Place the veal in the center of the platter. Quickly boil down the liquid in the casserole by half and strain over the vegetables. Garnish with chopped parsley.

† *VENISON STEAKS WITH CUMBERLAND SAUCE*

8 venison steaks	2 tbsp lemon juice
butter	½ tsp dry mustard
salt and pepper	½ tsp grated onion
CUMBERLAND SAUCE	¼ tsp powdered ginger
grated rind of 1 orange	⅔ cup port wine
grated rind of ½ lemon	8 oz red currant jelly
½ cup orange juice	

Have the steaks cut from the loin of well-hung venison. Brush them with melted butter and sprinkle with salt and pepper. Broil or pan-broil, allowing 5 to 6 minutes on each side. Serve with hot Cumberland sauce.

CUMBERLAND SAUCE: Combine all the ingredients in an enamel or stainless steel pan, and stir over moderate heat until the jelly melts.

† *LEEKS VINAIGRETTE*

2 to 3 bunches of leeks
Vinaigrette Sauce (see page 259)
chopped parsley

Choose leeks that are not too large. Allow 3 or 4 to a serving. Remove most of the green, and trim off the root ends. Wash very carefully to remove all the sand. Boil gently in salted water for 30 to 40 minutes or until tender. Drain and cool. Place in a deep, nonmetal serving platter, and pour the vinaigrette sauce, made with white wine vinegar, over them. Sprinkle with chopped parsley.

† *BAKED FENNEL*

Fennel has a strong flavor of anise much appreciated by the people living in the Mediterranean countries, and it is growing in popularity elsewhere. Baked in white sauce, its flavor is very mild and pleasant.

6 to 8 fennel	fine bread crumbs
White Sauce (page 259)	butter
2 tsp lemon juice	

Wash and trim the leaves from the fennel bulbs, and remove the outer layer of white. Cut them in quarters and cook 20 to 30 minutes in 3 cups of boiling salted water, or until just tender. Drain, but reserve the liquid. Make a well-seasoned cream sauce, using 1 cup of the cooking liquid and 1 cup of rich milk. Add the lemon juice. Arrange the fennel in a buttered heatproof serving dish. Cover with the cream sauce. Sprinkle with the bread crumbs, dot with butter, and bake in a 325° F oven for 25 minutes.

† *BROCCOLI EN PURÉE*

2 boxes chopped frozen broccoli	1½ cups milk, scalded
3 tbsp butter	⅛ tsp nutmeg
4 tbsp flour	½ tsp salt
	¼ tsp white pepper

Heat the broccoli in 1 cup of water just to the boiling point, breaking the frozen block with a fork. Drain. Put in a blender with the butter, flour, scalded milk, and spices. Spin for 1 minute. Place the mixture in the upper part of a double boiler and cook for 15 minutes over simmering water.

About 2 lbs fresh broccoli can be cooked 15 minutes in salted water, drained, and treated the same way, but unless it is garden fresh the frozen variety is equally good.

† CABBAGE IN CREAM

6 cups shredded cabbage   salt and pepper
4 tbsp butter   caraway seeds (optional)
½ pint cream

Cook the shredded cabbage in a large kettle of boiling, salted water for 6 to 8 minutes, or until *just* tender. Drain thoroughly, and reheat with the butter and cream without boiling. Season with salt and pepper, and add the caraway seeds if you like.

† NEW POTATOES IN HERB BUTTER

3 lbs small, new potatoes   2 tbsp chopped parsley
4 tbsp melted butter   salt and pepper
2 tbsp chopped chives

Scrub the potatoes but do not peel. Boil in salted water for 20 to 25 minutes or until tender. Drain and return to the pan. Shake the pan over medium heat to dry them well. Add the butter, herbs, salt, and pepper and serve very hot.

† MACÉDOINE OF VEGETABLES

4 cups of mixed vegetables:	celery
carrots	asparagus
white turnips	4 tbsp butter
shell beans	1½ tbsp sugar
artichoke hearts	2 cups White Sauce (page 259)
green beans	salt and pepper
wax beans	
peas	

Almost all vegetables are suitable for a macédoine except those of the cabbage family (which are too strong) and the leafy varieties. Traditionally the carrots and turnips are cut into thick sticks, and then the corners are rounded to give them a lozenge shape. If this takes too much time and patience, just cut the vegetables into as uniform a length and shape as possible. Boil the vegetables in salted water, starting with the harder varieties (carrots, turnips, shell beans, artichoke hearts), gradually adding the more tender varieties. This whole process should take 15 to 20 minutes if the water is kept boiling. Drain.

Heat butter in a large skillet. Add the vegetables and shake the pan so that any water left is evaporated and the vegetables get well coated with butter. Sprinkle with sugar and shake the pan again. Stir in the white sauce. Cover and simmer until the vegetables are all tender. Season with salt and pepper.

† PEAS IN HEAVY CREAM

6 lbs fresh green peas	3 tbsp butter
or 3 boxes frozen peas	½ pint heavy cream
1 tsp sugar	salt and pepper

Ideally peas should be picked, shelled, cooked, and served within an hour. If you can manage this, no sugar is needed, but most peas that come to the table are better for the sugar, whether fresh or frozen. Boil the peas in a small amount of water to which both sugar and salt have been added. Boil until just tender. Do not overcook. Drain, and reheat with butter and cream. Do not boil. Season with salt and pepper.

† JERUSALEM ARTICHOKE CHIPS

1 lb Jerusalem artichokes
fat
sea salt

Boil the Jerusalem artichokes in salted water until almost tender. Drain and peel off the skin. Dry them thoroughly. Slice very thin and dry them again. Fry them in deep fat at 365° F or in 2 inches of fat in a skillet, doing a small portion at a time. Drain on paper towels and sprinkle with sea salt.

† BOODLE'S ORANGE FOOL

1 sponge cake   ¼ cup sugar
2 large oranges   2 tbsp Cointreau
1 lemon   2 cups heavy cream

Cut the cake in inch-thick slices and place them in a large, shallow dessert dish. Combine the grated rind and juice of the oranges and lemon with the sugar and the Cointreau. Stir until the sugar dissolves. Beat the cream until thick but not stiff. Add the juice mixture, beating continuously. Pour this over the cake and chill in the refrigerator for 3 or 4 hours before serving.

† PEACH FLAN

Single Crust Dessert Pastry (page 260)
½ cup apricot jam
4 or 5 perfect peaches
½ cup sugar

2 tbsp Cointreau
   or apricot brandy
1 tbsp butter

Preheat the oven to 400° F. Place a buttered 8 inch flan ring on a baking sheet, and line with the pastry; or line an ordinary pie plate with the pastry. Cover the dough on bottom and sides with aluminum foil or heavy wax paper. Fill the shell half full of dried beans to keep the crust from rising. Bake 15 minutes. Remove the foil or paper and the beans, and keep them to use another time. Cool the shell and remove the ring.

Bring the jam to a boil stirring with a whisk. Paint the bottom of the crust with a thin layer of jam. Peel, stone, and slice the peaches. Overlap the slices in the shell in a concentric fashion. Sprinkle with sugar and liqueur and dot with butter. Bake 30 minutes at 350° F. Remove from the oven and brush with the rest of the jam. Cool on a wire rack.

† PLUM PUDDING

1 cup seedless raisins
1 cup golden seeded raisins
1 cup currants
1 cup sherry
½ cup brandy
6 eggs well beaten
½ lb chopped suet
3 cups soft bread crumbs

½ lb mixed, candied fruit peel,
   chopped
½ cup shredded almonds
2 tsp cinnamon
1 tsp ground ginger
1 tsp nutmeg
½ tsp ground cloves
¼ tsp salt
1¼ cups brown sugar

Soak the raisins and currants in the sherry and brandy for an hour, stirring occasionally. Combine with the remaining ingredients and mix thoroughly. Pack in a large, buttered melon mold or "pudding basin." Cover tightly and put on a trivet in a kettle that has 2 inches of water in the bottom. Cover and steam for 5 to 6 hours. Do not boil dry.

If the pudding is to be used immediately, unmold it and serve with one of the sauces. Otherwise, unmold the pudding, and let it cool. Wash the mold and line it with cheesecloth. Replace the pudding and sprinkle it liberally with brandy. Cover and store in a cool place. Before serving, steam it again for 1 to 2 hours. Pour hot brandy over it and ignite it.

† CUSTARD SAUCE

2 cups milk	2 eggs
⅛ tsp salt	1 tsp vanilla
6 tbsp sugar	1 tbsp brandy

Scald the milk with the salt and sugar. Pour gradually over the well-beaten eggs, beating continously. Cook in the top of a double boiler over simmering water, stirring until thick. Add the vanilla and brandy. Cool.

† HARD SAUCE

½ cup softened butter	1 tbsp brandy
1½ to 2 cups confectioners' sugar	¼ tsp nutmeg
⅛ tsp salt	

Mix all the ingredients except the nutmeg with an electric beater or by hand, using enough sugar to make a firm paste. If it becomes too crumbly, add a little cream. Pack in a small, decorative mold and chill. Unmold it on a small plate and dust very lightly with nutmeg.

† ROYAL ENGLISH TRIFLE

6 eggs	1 cup sherry
½ cup sugar	1 cup shredded almonds
3 cups milk, scalded	1 dozen small Italian macaroons
3 tsp vanilla	candies cherries
36 lady fingers	angelica
strawberry jam	¾ pint whipping cream
	½ cup confectioners' sugar
	almonds

Beat the eggs and sugar until light. Add the milk gradually, beating constantly. Add 2 tsp vanilla. Place in the top of a double boiler and stir over simmering water until slightly thickened and the sides of the pan are coated. Pour into a bowl and cool.

Split the lady fingers and spread them with the jam. Re-form them, and place a layer in the bottom of a deep glass dessert dish. Sprinkle with sherry and a few almonds and cover with a coating of the custard. Using this as a base, alternate split lady fingers and macaroons around the bowl, rounded sides out. Add another layer of lady finger sandwiches. Sprinkle again with sherry, almonds, and a layer of custard. Ring the surface with halves of candied cherries and angelica cut in small diamond shapes. Repeat the whole process, using your fancy in decoration. Finish with a layer of lady fingers well sprinkled with sherry. Chill overnight in the refrigerator. To serve, cover with heaps of sweetened whipped cream using confectioners' sugar and flavored with 1 tsp vanilla. Top with cherries, angelica, and almonds.

† SCOTCH WOODCOCK
(4 servings)

6 eggs	butter
1 cup cream	anchovy paste
4 slices firm white bread	anchovy fillets

Beat the eggs and cream until well blended. Toast the bread.

Spread with butter and a thin film of anchovy paste. Put on individual plates and keep warm.

Heat 2 tbsp butter in a skillet. Pour in the egg mixture and stir gently with a wooden spoon until thick and creamy. Season very sparingly. Spread the eggs over the toast and crisscross with anchovy fillets.

TEN

In a Manner of Speaking

Lord Peter said, "Hah. . . ." Lord Peter said, "Umph. . . ."
Lord Peter said, "Ah!"
                           DOROTHY L. SAYERS, *Unnatural Death*

Aristocrats, young and old, have the art of minimal language
down pat. They drawl. They slur. They slide. In their vagary,
they trail away mid-sentence, and often fail to make it through a
word. The same want of energy that causes their bodies to fall
into languid postures against the fireplace, or makes their eye-
lids droop, appears to paralyze their tongues. Final consonants
are the first freight to be pitched. This habit of nonspeech is
partly inherited from their guv'nor, who can't talk at all. What
speech the young men manage is remarkably fatuous, as P. J.
Wodehouse documented conclusively.

The same exhaustion overcomes the brain itself, when a
word eludes it. The effort of searching out the word in the musty
corridors of the mind being far and away too much, the problem
is circumvented by expressions such as "thing-ma-jig," by insub-

stantial words such as "thing," or by letting the listener fill in the blanks, as in "what-d'you-call-it," thus tossing the ball into the other chap's court.

Among the practitioners of minimal language, the Dotty Duchess, like her husband and son, is superb. Her vocabulary is, at the top, fifteen words, liberally muddled and dithered; the rest of her conversation is done by inflection. "Oh, I *say!*"— alarmed disgust after being told what the spaniel did that afternoon. "*Oh*, I say." Prolonged "oh," and "I say" diminished to indicate the last degree of sympathy to another matron at tea, whose future son-in-law has announced his intention of going into the ministry. The beleaguered lady will respond dolefully, "He's quite nice, really," believing the reverse to be true, in an obvious attempt to convince herself.

When Her Ladyship calls her husband "darling," her voice is light with patience and love; when she speaks to one of her children, her voice tinkles as if she were talking to diamonds. With a true English distaste for extravagance and showiness, she says the house, or the play, or the baby is "rather sweet," "rather beastly," or "rather a bore," as the case may be. Yet, when she cheers, she dips lavishly into enthusiasm. "Jolly good!" "Marvelous!" Or she responds gaily to a need to pawn her emeralds with, "Such fun, darling!" Conversely, "Poor you" covers every shade of commiseration.

Evidently the culpability of emotion and the inclination of words to reveal it, have gone far in silencing the entire nation. Poirot remarks in Agatha Christie's *Murder in the Calais Coach*, "The more emotional they feel, the less command they have of language." Understatement, splendid self-restraint, the terse condemnation are obvious results. When, in Ngaio Marsh's *Deadly Duo*, the heroine says, "You haven't been terribly clever, Victor. I shan't forgive you," she manages to remain a lady, inhumanly cool and murderously scathing on almost nothing.

One of the most highly developed means of communication is the cough. The cough has suffered an apparent decline in popularity, which is a loss. In its heyday, it added its own texture to the polyphony of dialects and drawls, of allusive mumbles and banal exclamations of the mystery genre. In fact, it said something. The cough has been used successfully by the velvet-footed butler to announce his presence, lest he overhear something. (A possibility, which if he is wise, he fights against mightily. See consequences otherwise in Chapter 12, "The Butler: What He Saw.") The frequently cadaverous or gloomy mien of a butler, coupled with the cough, should not cause one to conclude he is not in health. By no means. The cough is the signal of his perfect discretion. The clearing up of the cough has left little but oily silence for butlers, during which time they must occupy themselves with surely less fulfilling, because less expressive, silent but telling, scrutinies of the quality of labels in one's hat or coat.

A cough can apologize for the presumptuousness of an intrusion. From the butler it may suggest, "I would have handled it otherwise, my lord." It can be used by a brash inspector like a trumpet before an announcement. It can be employed Above Stairs by gentlemen suffering acute embarrassment, as a diversion while a friend blows his brains out, or by friends who, realizing another gentleman's embarrassment, tactfully cough for him. The cough is no end useful.

When you consider the frightful silences that spell reprimand, the restraint and detachment that are virtues, the virtue of being economical, the dislike of showiness—material, spiritual, or emotional—it's a wonder, and a blessing (for where would our mystery books be?) the English speak at all. Eea?

ELEVEN

The Staff

The truth is that the ancient world was more familiar with its slaves than the modern world with its servants.

G. K. CHESTERTON, "On Domestic Servants"

The importance of the green baize door cannot be overstressed. It serves as a barrier to muffle the shrieks of the hysterical housemaids till they can be brought under control. More significantly, like the staircase which serves to keep people in their places, the green baize door stands as a psychological barrier between the servants' hall and the rest of the house. It is yet another aspect of the situation Chesterton remarked in "On Domestic Servants": "Victorian ladies and gentlemen sniffed over their fierce feudal ancestors whose servants dined below the salt, while their own servants dined below the floor. They would never have dreamed of tolerating a housemaid at the other end of their own table, but kept her in a kind of cavern under the pavement."

Like high church and low, high tea and low, Above Stairs and Below, the staff itself is divided into upper and lower servants. A lower servant is barely visible. He has a forelock which he pulls like a bell rope in deference to every gentleman he sees, and he bobs before, after, and during speech. The effect of both is anonymous, and dizzying. One could have a servant about the place for years and never recognize him standing still or with the hair brushed back from his face. Should either occur, one would discover in a second a remarkable resemblance to Lord Aston-Martin.

Most of a lower servant's efforts are bent on making himself scarce. Dashing off the scene behind a barrow that he has been sitting on to smoke a pipe, with the speed of a startled deer, should the master's motor toot at the bend down the road. In these hyperactivities, the lower servant is not much distinguished from other servants; he simply has the advantage of more places to hide and lurk, and more territory to scamper across.

Upper servants have permanent dispositions inherited with their titles as, for example, sourness in housekeepers, irascibility in cooks, remoteness and dignity in butlers, rabbitiness in housemaids, feistiness in gardeners. Servants even inherit their names, in some cases, to avoid wear and tear on the already strained mental capacities of the master and mistress. Either the housekeeper or the butler is in charge of the upper servants, though in mysteries, in an establishment of any size, it is usually the butler.

Housekeepers may be recognized by the long, black dresses they wear, and the gold watch pinned to their flat bosoms. Their dresses always rustle, which makes one think of taffeta, but even when they are print dresses housekeepers can manage to make them crackle with agitation. Housekeepers' faces are permanently sour and disapproving; they enjoy calamity. Housekeepers are guaranteed ugly, and wear their dark hair skinned back in a bun.

Like gardeners, housekeepers are often bullies, and spend as much time as a butler would intimidating the mistress. This is done by suggesting breakfast at eight-thirty or nine, for example, when the housekeeper knows full well the mistress is used to rising at nine-thirty, but will not have the courage to say so (more effective with young or timid mistresses). Housekeepers really prefer to be bullied and kept in their place; they are fond of the old ways. The preferred mistress draws her finger over tabletops to check for dust, looks under mats, does not allow the servants to use the telephone, and inquires after the remains of the chocolate soufflé. This is the way things are done in a gentleman's house.

Apart from running the house—and running out of it—the purpose of the staff in a mystery is to prove itself inferior. Almost every action must contribute a further example of cowardice, apathy toward veracity, perhaps a trifling tendency to steal, occasional recalcitrance on the part of the older, more established personnel, and increasing freshness of the young and new. Freshness is a sign of the times, and signifies the approaching end of an era, as Miss Marple or any other little old lady could tell you. Maids began getting above themselves, as their skirts got above their knees.

To make the aristocratic society function properly not only must the lower classes be lower, they must enjoy it and want to stay that way. It is altogether desirable to believe it natural for butlers to want to polish silver, and that maids are, at best, so silly they couldn't possibly aspire to a better life; that servants lack initiative and independence, and infinitely prefer a little stipend at the master's death, and the thought of retirement; that they are grateful to be in the Great House, protected as vassals of old. This way, one can keep them in their places without compunction.

Which is not to say that servants do nothing but argue the status quo, run the realities, and provide contrast for the excellence of the upper class by proving themselves inferior (although the best time for the staff to show its worst qualities is at the time of the murder). The truth is there is no element in the mystery more important than the staff. With their shrieks, they play Greek chorus to the tragic events Above Stairs, moaning delightedly over a funeral, screaming in Agatha Christie's *The Seven Dials Mystery* with "pleasurable excitement" at the sight of blood, rushing from one side of the house to the other till, if it were a boat, it would be in danger of capsizing. The staff is the flesh-and-blood equivalent of the leafy backgrounds and somber-walled settings, the human aspect of the inhuman atmosphere. The ambulatory position of the young housemaids, poised in flight between house and bus stop, entering rooms with dust cloths or tea trays, exiting with screams, gives the mystery much of its sense of movement; butler or housekeeper acting as ringmasters to so many petulant ponies.

In other ways, the staff has a lot of weight to throw around. They control the calendar for murder by their days on and off; their rising and setting is of more moment than the rising and setting of the sun. The accidents of their lives—whom they walk in on doing what—are far more crucial than those of the principal actors. Such incidents create the need to alter one's murder plans to include a maid or two. Left unattended to, a maid could cause a dénouement on the second page, if she but chose to open her mouth. With butler, maid, cook, and gardener in their expected places, doing and saying their expected things—but only then—a murder can go on.

TWELVE

The Butler: What He Saw

The whole place had the usual disconsolate early-morning look. What was worse, as they passed along the dusky gallery, he could have sworn he heard somebody sobbing in one of the rooms. Thompson had obviously noticed it, though he pretended otherwise. He said that there would be breakfast in half an hour. The man's swollen jaw (hadn't Bohun said something about a toothache?) was paining him, and the news of the murder must clearly have torn the last rags of his self-possession.

CARTER DICKSON, *The White Priory Murders*

It is the butler who suffers most in these affairs. The butler is usually discovered, when not opening the door to—"It's the police, Madam!"—behind the green baize door (as necessary to butlers as clocks to cuckoos), or hovering over a side table of steaming dishes. Because of his perambulatory and nocturnal habits, he may, and too often for his own welfare does, happen upon the murderer at a rather tight moment when the latter would have preferred not to be interrupted. Or he sees something compromising. Some of the duties which keep him abroad at night are: making sure the windows are closed, so that this action can be used to help establish the time of the crime, locking the door, ditto, and leaving whisky and sandwiches in the library for the murderer to diddle.

The cough, which has proved so effective for so many classes (see Chapter 10, "In a Manner of Speaking"), is the butler's chief means of communication. However, the butler can go one better, he can give answers by stiffening his reactionary, aristocratic spine. On duty and off, he wears the mask of the well-trained servant. He can estimate your finances from your umbrella, your breeding from your hatband.

Good butlers smuggle jellies and charlotte russe from the dining room to the children of the family; bad butlers make people feel small. Just how small is sized up by Michael Innes in *The Case of the Journeying Boy:* "The man slightly raised his eyebrows, as if to indicate his surprise that even one so uncouth as this caller should be ignorant of the conventions of admittance and exclusion. . . .

Cadover produced a card. 'I am a detective-inspector from Scotland Yard,' he said.

"'Indeed, sir.' Ever so faintly, the tone contrived to imply that some such melancholy fact had already been only too apparent."

The butler's age may range from middle to doddering and unless he is the murderer he has an impeccable sense of propriety no better exemplified than in himself. He is also gifted with an abiding sense of loyalty to the family, frequently rewarded by his own death, or by a legacy, in the event of the untimely demise of his employer, anywhere from fifty to a hundred pounds, and a good reference.

Often, when aristocratic families are threatened with losing their money in more than seeming, there is no thought that the retainers will drop their dust cloths mid-flourish, and hightail it for the bus stop the way they do when murder strikes. No,

Old Dodders will be more inclined to totter off to a shoebox hidden under his sagging mattress, and return to discreetly offer the master a fiver, or his life savings. Old retainers are like that. More family than family. Any offerings of this sort will be made in the most tasteful, moving, and humble way. Essentially, if you know Old Retainer psychology, you know they will work for nothing, out of loyalty. They might even pay you, if the chips were down.

The morning after the murder, while the family and weekend guests totter about upstairs washing away the effects, the butler must organize a staff preparing to bolt on the next bus between outbursts of hysterics or cowering below stairs with the nerves of rabbits and teeth to match. These insights into staff behavior give us to know, without quite spelling it out, the inherent weakness of the lower classes. Meanwhile, in the calmer atmosphere upstairs, death careers on unabated.

Murder generally occurs in the night to facilitate discovering the body first thing in the morning. This starts everyone's day with a bang, and sends them flying in all directions, until they remember it's time for breakfast, and stop mid-flight to head for the morning room.

After the crime, the household suffers, not from want of appetite, but from a certain delicacy in acknowledging it. Among those present at the board are sure to be the murderer, relatives and friends of the present victim, and an upcoming victim or two. The present victim is probably just down the hall in the library being measured and photographed. Yet, it is not grief or fear that cries halt to breakfast at eight. It is the rule of convenience. Thus, guest, near-victim or murderer, having adjusted the knot of his tie or pinched a little pink in her cheeks, as the case may be, and decided to go on, may come down at any time to a sideboard loaded as for a hunt breakfast (which, in effect, it is). Kidneys, kippers, toast, and tea are kept piping hot in silver dishes, Old Dodders standing by.

The butler must shift as best he can to present something palatable, yet not offensively robust, to the victims of the upset.

Also, no matter what he has endured, he must preserve the same outward calm as those upstairs, while still being able to translate their wishes to those below. This, despite the fact that he may himself have submitted to hours of grueling questioning by the police or the harassment of the police detective who keeps dodging into his pantry hoping to catch him off guard as he polishes the plate. Butlers always take an excruciating pleasure in polishing plate. It is a privilege for which they were born and bred.

The butler may also be in extreme personal danger because he has Seen Something. If he knows he's seen what he's seen, he must not let it slip or stand to ruin the family honor. If he doesn't know he knows, he'll get it anyway. Murderers have an almost stronger sense of propriety than butlers. They don't like to leave loose ends, and they never chance the odd fit of lucidity even in doddering butlers.

Frequently the butler is forced to lower himself to serving sandwiches and coffee to the police in the kitchen which is, of course, an offense to his delicate sense of propriety. Policemen fall between two stools, being neither part of the house nor guests, neither upstairs material nor Below Stairs occupants. The butler is always more sensitive to social irregularities than the family. While he cringes at the police treading private pathways, the family will, by the end of the book, blithely affiance their daughter, Lady Jane, to the police detective, who has little to recommend him but a strong chin and a tendency to surprise butlers in their pantries.

† *THE HUNT BREAKFAST*

Among those less murderously inclined, the same breakfast buffet may serve as a Sunday brunch. There are endless variations on the English breakfast: fried eggs, bacon, sausages, broiled tomatoes, kidneys, mushrooms, kippers, cold grouse,

York ham, fried bread, toast, marmalade, tea. The even more substantial Scottish breakfast can be drawn on in cold weather, or before a rugged outing. The English buffet is then increased to include: porridge, bannocks and honey, finnan haddie, and whisky in the tea. Scotch oatmeal—a finer grained, softer oatmeal—is traditionally served plain, but it grows less austere with the addition of brown sugar, butter, cream and sugar, honey, jam, golden syrup, if available, or whisky. Oatmeal is second only to tea in its ability to put starch into the faint-hearted.

HUNT BREAKFAST *(American Brunch)*
  Watercress Salad
  Breakfast Mixed Grill
  Kippered Herring and Herbed Scrambled Eggs
  Trout with Lemon Parsley Butter
  Kedgeree
  Toad in the Hole
  Sausages and Chestnuts
  Baps
  Ham-Filled Crêpes
  Bath Buns
  Scotch Brown Bread
  English Muffins

† *WATERCRESS SALAD*

2 bunches watercress   Vinaigrette Sauce (page 259)

Pick over the watercress, removing any wilted leaves and very coarse stems. Wash thoroughly and crisp in the refrigerator. Mix with vinaigrette sauce just before serving. Crumbled bacon may be added to this very refreshing, breakfast-time salad.

† BREAKFAST MIXED GRILL

A mixed grill takes organization when there are more than two or three people to be served because most home kitchens do not have broilers large enough to accommodate all the delicious ingredients. However, with the help of an electric frying pan or large skillet for pan-broiling some of the items, it is all quite simple.

16 large mushroom caps	8 lamb chops, 1 inch thick
olive oil	8 lamb kidneys
salt and black pepper	8 slices of bacon
4 firm tomatoes	16 precooked link sausages
sugar	toast
oregano	butter
	lemon wedges
	parsley

Wash the mushroom caps and dry them quickly with toweling. Place them in a small bowl with ¼ cup of olive oil, salt, and black pepper. Let stand 30 minutes.

Cut the tomatoes in half crosswise and gently squeeze out the seeds. Place them on a baking sheet. Brush them with olive oil, and sprinkle them with salt, pepper, a very little sugar and oregano. Let them stand.

Trim any excess fat from the chops. Remove the film and fatty core from the kidneys and split them in half.

Pan-broil the bacon and drain on paper toweling. Do the same with the sausages, and keep both bacon and sausages warm.

Grease the rack of the broiling pan and preheat the rack under the broiler. Place the chops on the hot rack and broil 3 inches away from the flame for 5 minutes. Turn the chops and add the kidneys and tomatoes. Broil 7 to 8 minutes. At the same time pan-broil the mushrooms 2 to 3 minutes on each side.

To serve: Place each chop on a piece of toast. Brush generously with soft butter and sprinkle with salt and pepper. Top each chop with 2 mushrooms and a slice of bacon, and surround the platter alternately with the kidneys, tomatoes, and sausages. Garnish with lemon wedges and sprigs of parsley.

† KIPPERED HERRING AND HERBED SCRAMBLED EGGS

2 7-oz cans kippered herring
butter
lemon juice
12 large fresh eggs
1¼ cups rich milk

12 tbsp butter
1 tbsp each chopped chives
  and parsley
1 tsp chopped tarragon
1½ tsp salt
½ tsp white pepper

Place the herring in a frying pan with some of the liquid from the cans. Dot with butter and sprinkle with lemon juice. Heat slowly.

Beat the eggs and milk until well blended. Cut the butter into small bits and mix into the eggs. Add the chopped herbs, salt, and pepper. Pour into a large, slightly heated skillet, and stir with a wooden spoon over moderate heat. Cook until creamy and thick.

Serve the eggs on a warm (not hot) platter surrounded by the kippered herrings.

† TROUT WITH LEMON PARSLEY BUTTER

8 trout (fresh or flash-frozen)
salt and white pepper
flour
8 tbsp butter

1½ tbsp chopped parsley
2 tsp lemon juice

Wipe the cleaned trout with toweling. (If frozen, they should be *just* thawed.) Sprinkle the inside with salt and white pepper. Coat lightly with flour mixed with a little salt and pepper. Heat 4 tbsp butter in 1 large or 2 medium sized skillets until it is hot and sizzling, but not burning. Place the trout in the butter and brown 4 to 5 minutes on each side depending on size.

Heat a platter and put the cooked fish on it. Quickly add the rest of the butter to the skillet. When very hot add the chopped parsley and lemon juice. Pour the herbed butter over the fish and carry to the table immediately. It should be sizzling loud enough to be heard.

† KEDGEREE

1 cup rice	cayenne
¾ lb finnan haddie°	1 egg
¼ lb butter	⅓ cup heavy cream
3 hard-boiled eggs, chopped	2 tbsp chopped parsley
salt	paprika
black pepper	

° 1 cup flaked salmon or cod may be substituted, if desired.

Wash the rice and boil it in salted water for 14 minutes. Drain and rinse it by letting cold water run through it in the drainer. Place in a baking dish and let it dry out in a 350° F oven for 20 minutes, fluffing it occasionally with a fork.

Meanwhile, poach the finnan haddie in water for 20 minutes or until flaky. Remove from water and flake the fish, removing any bones or hard parts. Heat the butter in a large saucepan. Add the fish and stir until well coated with the butter. Add the chopped hard-cooked eggs and the rice. Season to taste with salt, pepper, and cayenne. Beat the egg and cream together and stir the mixture into the rice and fish. The texture should be creamy. Serve immediately in a heated serving dish and sprinkle with the chopped parsley and paprika.

† TOAD IN THE HOLE

This dish can be partly prepared in advance and quickly finished the next morning.

2 lbs sausage meat	2 cups flour
4 eggs	1 tsp salt
2 cups milk	½ tsp baking powder

Make 2-inch patties about ½ inch thick of the sausage meat. Brown the patties in a very hot skillet for 3 minutes on each side. Drain the sausage on paper toweling. Spread 4 tbsp of the sausage fat in a heatproof serving dish large enough to accommodate the patties in a single layer and 2½ to 3 inches deep. Arrange the patties in the dish and keep in a cool place.

The next morning, preheat the oven to 425° F.

Heat the dish containing the sausages. At the same time, beat the eggs 3 minutes. Add the milk, flour, salt, and baking powder and beat just until blended. Pour the mixture over the sausages. It should just cover them. Bake 30 minutes and serve immediately.

† SAUSAGES AND CHESTNUTS

24 chestnuts	1 cup dry white wine
8 sausage patties	4 sprigs parsley
2 tbsp butter	½ bay leaf
3 tbsp flour	¼ tsp powdered thyme
3 cups bouillon	salt and pepper

Preheat oven to 450° F.

With a sharp pointed knife, make an X on the flat side of each chestnut. Place them on a baking sheet and bake for 10 minutes. Cool slightly and remove the outer shell and skin.

Brown the sausage patties in butter, turning them once. Remove the patties and drain them on toweling.

Remove all but 4 tbsp fat from the pan. Reheat and stir in the flour. When nicely browned, add the bouillon gradually and stir. Add the wine and, still stirring, bring to a boil. Add the parsley and bay leaf tied together and the thyme. Season the sauce with salt and pepper.

Place the chestnuts in a heavy covered casserole. Surround with the sausage and pour the sauce over everything. Cover and simmer for 1 hour. Remove the parsley and bay leaf and serve either in a chafing dish or in the dish in which it was cooked kept warm on a hot tray. This is particularly delicious when served with small baked apples.

† BAPS

4½ cups all-purpose flour	1 tsp sugar
4 tbsp butter or margarine	½ cup lukewarm water
2 packages dry yeast	1 cup nonfat milk

Combine the flour and butter with an electric beater or by rubbing them together with your hands. Dissolve the yeast and sugar in the warm water. Heat the milk until it is just lukewarm and add the dissolved yeast. Add this to the flour and butter mixture and stir until you have a soft dough. Cover and let rise at room temperature until it has doubled in size.

Turn the dough onto a floured surface and knead well. Shape into small oval buns. Place them on a floured baking sheet and let rise 15 to 20 minutes. Brush with milk and bake at 375° F. Serve with fresh butter and orange marmalade.

† HAM-FILLED CRÊPES

2 cups cake flour	½ lb cooked ham, diced
½ tsp salt	2 tbsp chopped onion
3 eggs	2 tbsp butter
2 cups nonfat milk	2 cups White Sauce (page 259)
6 tbsp salad oil	salt, pepper, and paprika
	½ cup grated cheese (medium Cheddar or Swiss)

Prepare the batter for the crêpes several hours in advance and let it stand in a cool place. Crêpes should be cooked in 5-inch heavy cast-iron pans reserved for this purpose. They require no greasing with this recipe and are wiped clean with paper towels.

Put the flour, salt, and eggs in a mixing bowl. Add ½ cup of milk and beat vigorously for 2 minutes. Add the rest of the milk gradually, beating continuously. The batter should be smooth and very thin. Add the oil. Just before cooking the crêpes, stir the batter well.

Cook the ham and onion in butter over moderate heat until the onion is soft. Make the white sauce and add 1½ cups of it to the ham. Season highly with salt, pepper, and paprika. Stir well and set aside.

To cook the crêpes, spoon about 1½ tbsp batter into a hot pan, moving the pan so that the batter covers the bottom. Cook over moderately high heat for about 60 seconds. Flip the crêpe over with a wide spatula, cook another minute or a little less and slide the crêpe onto a platter. With a little practice you can keep two pans going at once.

Put a generous tablespoon of the ham mixture on each crêpe. Wrap the crêpe around the mixture and place, seam side down, in a buttered heatproof serving dish. Spread a film of the remaining white sauce over the crêpes and sprinkle with the grated cheese. Bake in a 375° F oven until bubbling and light brown, about 10 minutes.

† BATH BUNS

4 cups all-purpose flour	⅔ cup sugar
1 tsp salt	3 eggs
2 packages dry yeast	½ cup yellow raisins
1 tsp sugar	½ cup candied fruit peel
½ cup lukewarm water	1 egg yolk
1 cup milk	2 tsp water
8 tbsp butter or margarine	sugar

Warm the flour mixed with salt in a medium oven for 5 minutes. Dissolve the yeast and sugar in the lukewarm water, heat the milk to lukewarm and add yeast mixture. Add this to the flour in a mixing bowl. Mix well and knead with the hands until well blended.

In another mixing bowl beat the butter until it is creamy, adding the sugar gradually. Beat the eggs into the butter and sugar one by one and when well blended add the raisins and half the candied peel. Combine the two mixtures and mix well. Cover and let rise at room temperature until doubled in size, about 45 minutes.

Knead the dough down and divide into round rolls. Place on a buttered baking sheet. Brush with the egg yolk blended with the water. Sprinkle with sugar and the rest of the candied peel. Bake 20 to 25 minutes at 350° F.

† *SCOTCH BROWN BREAD*

6 cups whole wheat flour	1 package dry yeast
1½ cups boiling water	½ cup lukewarm water
¼ cup dark brown sugar	1 tsp white sugar
2 tbsp butter or margarine	

This is a heavy, hearty bread. Using half white flour makes it lighter, but then it is no longer Scotch brown bread.

Warm the flour in a moderate oven. Pour the boiling water into a large mixing bowl containing the brown sugar and the shortening. Let cool until it is lukewarm. Dissolve the yeast in ½ cup lukewarm water with the white sugar and let stand for 5 minutes. Mix this in with the liquid in the mixing bowl along with 2 cups of the flour. Beat hard for 2 minutes. Add 3 more cups of flour and mix well. The dough should be soft, but firm enough to form a ball. Add more flour if necessary.

Turn the dough onto a lightly floured surface. Wash the bowl, dry it thoroughly, and grease it lightly. Knead the dough until it is very smooth and almost glossy. Place it in the bowl, turning it around so that it will be greased all over. Cover with a towel and let it rise until it has doubled in size. Punch it down and let it rise again for 45 minutes. Turn it out on the working surface and cut it in two. Let it rest for about 10 minutes. Then knead each portion and shape into 2 loaves. Put in greased bread pans, cover and let rise again until it has doubled. Bake one hour at 400° F.

† *ENGLISH MUFFINS*

Homemade English muffins are incomparably better than the American store variety. Follow the directions for making Crumpets found on page 30 substituting 5 cups of flour and 3 cups of the milk. The same method of preparation is used.

THIRTEEN

The Maid

"She knew something. . . ." "She's been upset, so the cook says, ever since Mrs. Symmington's death, and according to this Rose, she's been getting more and more worried, and kept saying she didn't know what she ought to do."
                    AGATHA CHRISTIE, *The Moving Finger*

Of all the incompetents in this world, maids must be the worst. Their want of brains is almost as great as their want of nerve (see Chapter 12, "The Butler: What He Saw"). It is necessary, for example, for Miss Marple to admonish a maid not to put the frilled, monogrammed sheets in the fire while warming them. She wouldn't even attempt to put across the art of airing a bed. She does it herself. Maids are as shallow and superficial in their way as great beauties are in theirs, and at the first hint of trouble they fly.

Maids come in all kinds, but only one shape, thin; and scared. There are chambermaids, housemaids, parlor maids, and 'tweenies—all usually young. Maids' duties are very narrowly prescribed: they draw drapes in the morning, bring in the tea, and discover bodies. After that, they spend the remainder of their time, with Elizabeth in Dorothy Sayers's *Five Red Herrings,* "hesitating whether to shriek or run away."

Without maids, murders could not take place. First, they are needed, like bloodhounds, to unearth the body. Second, and more important, who, if not the maid, would overhear something, but keep it to herself because it puzzled her? Who would see something without realizing what she saw? Who would, therefore, find herself being killed? Be simple enough to be lured to a deadly, forest picnic, as in Dorothy Sayers's *Unnatural Death,* by a sandwich of "coal-black, treacle-cured Bradenham ham"? Be stuffed, with the fishing rods and golf clubs, in the cupboard under the stairs for looking out the pantry window on what should have been her afternoon off? If, in addition, her name is Gladdie, her chances of survival are practically nil. Not that they're much better if her name is Evelyn, Flora, Clara, Edna, or Edith.

The only maid who has a fair chance of survival is the ladies' maid. She is a case apart; she is older, and may be intelligent. The ladies' maid comes with the mistress, and is directly responsible only to her. When the mistress travels, the ladies' maid is folded up in the luggage, and unfolds, ironing.

A ladies' maid is either hopelessly ugly, with a little mustache, or foreign, therefore hard and scheming. Her mouth, according to Ngaio Marsh in *Death of a Peer* seems to be forming the words "not quite nice" in perpetuity. Her life is spent in drawing delicious-smelling baths, putting away precious lingerie after mending it, laying out the white moire and diamonds for a party, with delighted fingers, and sitting upright in train compartments holding scarlet morocco cases filled with priceless rubies. Often ladies' maids are so loyal and possessive of their mistresses—frequently rich and beautiful, if not actually actresses—that they become confused about who's who, and kill one of their lady's young rivals. Or are jealous and beastly to the actress's lovers.

Ladies' maids spend most of their time in and around closets, when not hovering behind their mistress at the dressing table, so that she may chortle with pleasure, looking in the mirror, at the ugliness of the maid's face contrasted with the beauty of her own. This kind of vainglorying in someone else's defects can set up a shallow, superficial beauty (they all are) for an entire morning, until her first spray of orchids or diamonds comes from an admirer. At which point, she will hang the maid up in the closet, and go, alluringly peignoired in heavy lace, to receive in her sitting room. Should the lady die in transit, the ladies' maid changes her gray traveling gloves to black suède mourning ones.

An ordinary maid is, of course, given to gossip. Fortunately. Otherwise, no one would know that she knows something, and she might survive. For a maid to survive would bring about a fatal imbalance in a mystery book. If three people are murdered, one of them *must* be the maid.

If she knows she knows something, the maid will be quiet just the same. As she walks out with the fishmonger's boy, or the grocer's boy, or the butcher's boy—a social pattern which figures importantly in mysteries—there will be a stolen moment. A stolen moment takes place where it shouldn't, at a time when it oughtn't, between the maid and the boy she walks out with, which is a lip-sealer. Because the moment has been stolen from her work, the maid can't tell what she saw or heard.

When she isn't actually fainting or shrieking, the maid stammers and blushes unmercifully. Should she get enough of a grip on herself to attempt articulation, she further frustrates everyone by squeaking out that "she didn't ought to," or some such engagingly ungrammatical phrase. In order to get that much from her, she must be cajoled. Even when she hasn't stolen a moment, she is in fear and trembling of Cook, or some other Below Stairs worthy whose response, the maid feels dimly sure, will be a large dose of wrath. The master and mistress are too far beyond her comprehension even to be frightening. She would as lief confide in the murderer, and often does. Should she say her little piece to the police, however, it will not, strictly speaking, be true. Maids love their little drama.

Maids love their little drama so much that an unendangered maid, who was a friend of the maid who-didn't-realize-what-she-knew (past tense), will try for a moment in the limelight by telling several variations of the truth, rolling her eyes, clutching her heart and saying she's come all over queer this morning. To make clear how queer, she will have been unable to touch a morsel of seed cake. That *is* serious.

Should a policeman arrive at the front door, a maid will be incapable of babbling more than "Oh, please, ma'am, there's a policeinspectorhere,andhesayshemustspeaktoyou" before, in all probability, dropping in her tracks. It is unfortunate that maids are as thin as they are. They must be blue with bruises.

Maids are dead set against speaking to the police until they are forced; it comes with the equipment. This obscure, prehensile instinct will cause the police to shake their heads, as they do in Agatha Christie's *The Moving Finger*, and remark, "They've got that deep-seated prejudice against 'being mixed up with the police.' If she'd come along and told us what was worrying her, she'd be alive today." The book would also be over. Far better for the maid to telephone a housekeeper she used to be in service under, so that she can be overheard and dispatched.

A maid's world is completely restricted by the green baize door; the clock (she must be in by ten); and the days of the week (one day off a week, and alternate Sundays). Her close relationships are with other servants; the house itself is more in the nature of a museum she is allowed to visit regularly with a dust mop. Maids are often interrelated by blood, which speeds the flow of news from house to house.

When maids dream, they dream of a good place. A good place must be in town. If it is not, it must be near a bus stop, and they will want higher wages, or not come at all. The tone of the family must be up to her standards (a maid has her pride) and, in their dealings with her, the family must be generous and fair —giving her ample days off, letting her walk out, and allowing her to have her friends in to tea in the kitchen. The family should be able to look after itself, so that the maid is not overworked, and be polite to her (a maid has her feelings). Maids cry a lot. At the first hint of nastiness, the maid will be waiting at the bus stop, cheap old suitcase in hand, ready and waiting to be killed.

FOURTEEN

Nannies:
Order in the Court

"I thought you spoke of a nurse, my lord."

"Oh—you mean Nanny," said Lord Charles who now seemed to have himself very well in hand. "Yes, of course there's Nanny. We don't think of her as one of the servants."

"No, my lord?"

"No. She's the real head of affairs, you see."

NGAIO MARSH, Death of a Peer

Nannies are special cases. They are at war with Cook, to whom they have not spoken for years, and locked in a power struggle with the mistress, which will continue after the children have grown up, married, and moved away. The mistress is invariably the loser. Nannies belong in the Merry Old Dragon category when they are nice, but more frequently they are just plain dragons. They rule the entire household with an iron hand. Nanny must be kept happy or she will get even, and no one has better weapons. She may threaten to leave, posing the problem of the children falling ill from nightmares or broken hearts because they are perversely attached to her. And a mistress knows that if this nanny has faults, another nanny will simply mean an adjustment to a new set of faults. Besides, mothers grow frantic at the thought of coping with the little monsters Nanny has been carefully training to become guerrillas.

A nanny often stays with the children till they are well into middle age. If so, she is fiercely loyal. So much so, she is often a suspect, as she will go quite far in defense of "her child." Nanny makes the entire family drink Ovaltine before going to bed. She also has her own electric stove in the nursery, which lets her be as independent as she is with Cook. Nannies are as near as we come to the ancient crones huddling in the woods, gnarled fingers grasping spoons and stirring cauldrons, only today they play endless rounds of patience. Nanny knows more than she should know of the affairs of the family, and comments accordingly with a complete want of restraint.

Nanny knows little folkloric things like how to gauge the condition of your liver by the color of your tongue. The more a Nanny may love her charges, the more honor bound she is not to let it show lest she let down the entire nation. Nanny is relied upon to raise stout men of oak with stiff upper lips, who will evermore eschew the soft.

FIFTEEN

Crime in the Kitchen

"... which reminds me, I must go and see Mrs. Medway. Funny how servants cannot bear the police. Her cheese *soufflé* last night was quite uneatable. *Soufflés* and pastry always show if one is off balance. If it weren't for Gudgeon keeping them all together, I really believe half the servants would leave."

AGATHA CHRISTIE, *Murder After Hours*

Every cook in an English mystery seems to have trained under the cook in *Alice's Adventures in Wonderland*, who leaves off stirring her cauldron of highly peppered soup to hurl fire-irons, saucepans, plates, and dishes at her Lady Duchess. Cooks are temperamental beyond belief, despite the fact that artistry, such as might heat a French chef, doesn't often come into boiling potatoes or the rest of the relatively plain cooking cooks are employed to do. Cooks are suitably roly-poly from tasting and sampling, but despite the common belief that this should provide them with a jolly disposition, they are incredibly surly; just one more dragon around the house for the mistress to be intimidated by. Perhaps cooks are dyspeptic. Perhaps this is why English cooking suffers a want of reputation. Too many cranky cooks. Either their crankiness is making their cooking bad, or the badness of their cooking is making them cranky.

Cooks, their tempers and faces glowing like the kitchen fires, spend all day in the kitchen stirring, salting, popping in Yorkshire puddings, and the like. From time to time, they drop into a chair to have a cup of sweet, inky tea and a bit of a gossip with members of the staff free from their duties for a moment, while the tea kettle bubbles, and a pot of something substantial sputters on the stove. Cooks are always mid-feud, generally, with the nanny. Nannies are demanding, and put on airs; they can make special food requests at odd hours, and complain that the dishes didn't arrive hot.

After a poisoning, the cook has her moment. It is, of course, a ticklish one, fraught with the possibility that she will fly off the handle at the suggestion that anything could go wrong in her kitchen. One thing sure to make the cook even more irascible than usual is the descent of the police. Like any self-respecting servant, she has an innate mistrust of the police, and when she finds them in her bailiwick, dusting a flour tin for fingerprints, lifting lids, sniffing soups, taking away samples in little glass jars from the stone jars in the larder, she turns wrathful, and bangs pots and pans. She does this as a rule anyway. It puts off any member of the family who happens to be anywhere near the green baize door and might have wistful aspirations to a better life—or cuisine—and be about to voice them. Cooks are not just temperamental and noisy, they are conscientiously noisy, and, heaven knows, they are equipped for it.

Questioning by the police shows up immediately in the total inedibility of the evening meal. Frequent inedibility of the food due to choleric cooks compensates for the rather starchy diet of the English, so that they are not enormously overweight.

The police are not interested in the cook as a suspect, which might suit her resentful state better; they want to know how someone was poisoned. What was the cause? The mushrooms? The chicken? Who ate it? How much of it did the servants eat? For, like tasters for the kings of old, the staff stands ready to prove—by eating what is sent back to the kitchen from the table, and prospering—that there was nothing wrong with soup, fish, meat, sweet, savory. Process of elimination. On different levels. Even the cat casts a ballot.

One of the most carefully chronicled meals in mystery lore is the fatal dinner in Dorothy Sayers's *Strong Poison*. The problem is: Was the victim, Philip Boyes, murdered, or did he die of natural causes? The answer lies in a carefully cracked egg, injected with arsenic. But to get at this one fact, the entire book is strewn with recapitulations and examinations of the meal. For loving analysis, it is on a par with the famous dissection of the preparation of *boeuf en gelée* in Marcel Proust's *Within a Budding Grove*.

To discover the means by which the poison was introduced to the meal, Lord Peter Wimsey's man, Bunter, takes up his chair Below Stairs. Nowhere more than as accomplice *de la cuisine* is the full range of Bunter's resourcefulness seen. By and through the kitchen, Bunter helps Wimsey bait his traps. If Wimsey arrives home with a quarry, Bunter vibrates with sensibilities. Not a word, and out comes the priceless port, or the dish that turns the trick. Words tumble over each other. Confessions are mounted. A young doctor pours out a tale of unnatural death. Or a poisoner enjoys a trial by Turkish delights.

But Bunter in a strange kitchen is even better Bunter. Investigating the *Strong Poison* case, he sits sipping tea at the kitchen table, doffing his superiority with skillful ease in favor of an open and matey manner. When investigation delves to the delicate area Below Stairs—and we know how the servants feel about it's-the-police-madam, and how embarrassed they can be by the gentry—enter Bunter, triumphant. Quickly he disarms the occupants with unrestrained buttering of the crumpets. Gradually he gains their confidence through that most sensitive of all exchanges, the exchange of recipes. Finally, as his target is the cook (who knows something she doesn't know she knows), he has to forget his elevated tastes and be satisfied with going to a prayer meeting at the local chapel; indeed, give the lady hope that conversion is just a hymn away. The exchange between himself and the cook, Mrs. Pettican, is that of two empassioned professionals, who heed each other with the courteous grace of two martial dukes drawing up a treaty.

The police, on the other hand, require coffee. Not only that, if an investigation is prolonged, and it is necessary for several of them to stay on the spot to direct traffic in the corridors and stand guard at the scene of the crime, they will need food, as well. Which means another burden on the cook. The rest of the staff, after spending the first few hours cowering, will emerge from the shadows and corners to enjoy the novelty the police present. It will add cachet to their chats at neighboring houses. But the cook remains truculent at the invasion, and complains mightily if anyone will listen, or can hear, while crockery clatters and pots fall from the wall.

† THE ALL-DAY BUFFET

The All-Day Buffet makes murder possible. By providing food at all hours of the day and night, the buffet allows the family and guests to dodge in and out of the dining room between quick trips to London to see their solicitors or, if they are completely housebound, to come in after rigorous questioning by the police. The murderer, once more busy elsewhere, need not interrupt himself unnecessarily to make an appearance at a formal meal when he would rather be tidying up—getting rid of witnesses or clues. Because of the state of the staff, the All-Day Buffet should be easy to serve; because it is to be served to the police, who are more accustomed to eating meat pies and steak and chips in pubs, it must be simple, hearty fare.

THE ALL DAY BUFFET
(for six to eight people)
   Mulligatawny Soup
   Balmoral Soup
   Chafing Dish Lobster Thermidor
   Cold Smoked Tongue with Horseradish Cream
   Irish Lamb Stew
   Single Crust Milton Mowbray Pork Pie
   Shepherd's Pie
   Veal Kidneys in Dijon Souce
   Sautéed Potato Balls
   Wilted Cucumbers
   Lentil Salad
   Apple and Blackberry Tart
   Summer Pudding
   Treacle Tart

† *MULLIGATAWNY SOUP*
  (hot or cold)

1 cup boiling water	1 large onion, chopped
½ cup grated coconut	1 clove garlic, minced
1½ quarts beef stock or	½ apple, cored and sliced
canned bouillon	2 tbsp butter
½ tsp ground cardamom	1½ tbsp flour
8 peppercorns	2 tsp curry powder
¼ lemon, sliced	

Pour the boiling water over the coconut, cover and let steep 30 minutes. Strain and press through cheesecloth to obtain coconut milk. Simmer the stock with the cardamom, peppercorns, and lemon for 30

minutes. Cook the onion, garlic and apple in the butter in a large saucepan over low heat until soft. Add the flour and curry powder, and continue cooking 3 minutes, stirring constantly.

Strain the stock into the saucepan with the cooked apple and stir
well. Simmer 20 to 30 minutes and then add the coconut milk.

If served hot, cooked rice may be added. If cold, add ½ pint
heavy cream.

† *BALMORAL SOUP*

This is a "Scotch" way to use the bones of a roast of lamb.

¼ cup barley	1 cup diced turnips
lamb bones	1 cup diced carrots
1 onion	3 tbsp butter
1 carrot	4 tbsp flour
¼ tsp thyme	1 quart milk
1 bay leaf	croutons
4 to 6 sprigs of parsley	
salt and pepper	

Soak the barley in water for several hours. Cover the lamb bones,
which should have some meat left on them, with cold water, and bring
to a boil. Skim off any scum that comes to the top. Add the onion, carrot, herbs, and salt and pepper. Cover and simmer for three hours.
Strain. Cook down to 1 quart. Cool and chill. Remove any fat that
comes to the top. Cut off any meat from the bones, and save it.

Cook the diced vegetables in the broth until tender. In a saucepan
melt the butter and stir in the flour, letting it brown slightly. Add 2 cups
of milk and stir until smooth. Add the rest of the milk and, when hot,
add to the broth with the vegetables and any pieces of meat from the
bones. Add the barley and cook for 15 minutes. Taste and season highly
with salt and pepper. Serve with a side dish of croutons made by frying
small pieces of bread in butter.

† CHAFING DISH LOBSTER THERMIDOR

1 quart dry white wine	¾ lb mushrooms
1 quart water	10 tbsp butter
1 medium sized onion	8 tbsp flour
1 medium sized carrot	½ cup brandy
celery leaves	1½ cups heavy cream
3 or 4 sprigs parsley	1 tbsp Dijon mustard
1 bay leaf	3 egg yolks
¼ tsp thyme	½ lemon
8 peppercorns	salt, pepper, cayenne
4 2-lb lobsters (live)	chopped parsley

Combine the wine and water in a large kettle. Prepare and slice the vegetables thinly and add them with the herbs and peppercorns to the kettle. Cover and simmer for 20 minutes. Add the live lobsters, and when the water comes to a boil again, cook about 15 minutes or until, when you pick up one of the lobsters by a leg and give it a little shake, the leg detaches easily from the body. Remove the lobsters and boil down the broth until it measures 3½ to 4 cups. Strain the broth into a pan and set aside.

Meanwhile, trim, wash, and dry the mushrooms. Slice them. Cook covered in 2 tbsp butter until they are almost dry and set aside.

In the top part of a double boiler heat 8 tbsp butter and stir in the flour, stirring with a wooden spoon for 2 to 3 minutes over direct low heat without letting it brown. Stir in the broth in which the lobsters were cooked and continue cooking until smooth and creamy. Add the brandy and ½ cup of the cream. Simmer 2 minutes more and set aside.

Split the lobsters down the middle lengthwise. Remove the meat from the claws and tail and cut into bite-size pieces. Remove the green liver (tomale) and reserve.

Whisk the rest of the cream, the mustard, and the egg yolks together until well blended. Add the green liver from the lobsters and continue whisking. Pour in a little of the hot sauce, beating rapidly. Combine gradually with the rest of the sauce in the top of the double boiler and cook over hot water until thick and creamy. Add the lobster meat and the mushrooms and heat 15 minutes longer. Season well with lemon juice, salt, and pepper and a dash of cayenne. Transfer to a chafing dish and garnish with the feelers and chopped parsley.

† COLD SMOKED TONGUE WITH HORSERADISH CREAM

1 smoked tongue (approx.
  4 lbs)
1 bay leaf
6 sprigs parsley
celery leaves
1 onion, sliced
1 carrot, sliced
6 peppercorns

HORSERADISH CREAM
½ cup fresh grated horseradish, or
⅔ cup bottled horseradish
1 cup heavy cream, whipped
1½ tsp sugar
½ tsp salt

2 cucumbers

Cover the tongue with cold water. Tie the bay leaf, parsley, and celery leaves into a little bouquet, and put it in the kettle along with the onion, carrot, and peppercorns. Bring it to a boil slowly, removing any scum that rises to the surface. Cover and simmer 3 to 3½ hours or until tender when a fork is inserted in the thickest part. Cool in the broth. Slit the skin with a sharp knife and peel it off. Cut away the bones and the fat and gristle.

Combine the ingredients for the horseradish cream and chill in the refrigerator. Score and slice the cucumbers quite thin.

Slice the tongue thin and place in overlapping slices on a platter surrounded by the cucumber slices. Serve the horseradish sauce separately.

† IRISH LAMB STEW

3 lbs boned shoulder of lamb
10 large potatoes
6 or 7 onions
2 bay leaves
6 large sprigs of parsley

small bunch of celery leaves
¼ tsp thyme
salt and pepper
2 tbsp chopped parsley

Cut the meat in slices ¼ inch thick, trimming off most of the fat. Peel and cut the potatoes and onions in thick slices. Arrange the meat and vegetables in layers in a large, heavy pan with a tight-fitting cover.

Tie the bay leaves, parsley, and celery leaves into a small bouquet and lay it on top. Sprinkle with the thyme, salt, and freshly ground pepper. Add enough water to come just to the top of the contents of the pan. Bring to a boil over moderate heat, removing any scum that comes to the surface. Cover and simmer very slowly for approximately 2 hours. The potatoes should absorb almost all the water, giving the stew a thick consistency.

Remove the herb bouquet. Taste for seasoning. Serve in a heated dish. Sprinkle generously with chopped parsley and surround with Devils on Horseback (page 12).

† SINGLE CRUST MELTON MOWBRAY PORK PIE

5-lb pork loin roast	1½ cups all-purpose flour
1 tbsp salt	1 tsp salt
1 large onion, sliced	6 tbsp vegetable shortening
1 carrot, sliced	2 tbsp cold water
1 bay leaf	freshly ground black pepper
¼ tsp thyme	1 tbsp gelatine
6 peppercorns	

Place the pork, salt, onion, carrot, bay leaf, thyme, and peppercorns in a kettle. Fill ¾ full with cold water. Bring to a boil and cook gently for 2½ hours. Remove the meat from the kettle, and boil down the liquid until it measures about 2½ cups. Cool both meat and liquid and store in the refrigerator overnight.

Cut the shortening into the flour and salt, using a pastry blender, 2 knives, or a single electric beater. Add enough water to make the dough stick together. Knead it for a moment or two and cover. Let it rest at least 30 minutes.

Remove the meat and fat from the bones and cut in 1 inch pieces. Defat the liquid and warm it. Season highly, especially with pepper.

Fill a 1½ quart casserole with the meat and fat, moisten with a cupful of the liquid.

Preheat the oven to 425° F.

Roll out the pastry in a circle ¼ inch thick and 1½ inches wider than the diameter of the dish. Cut off a 1 inch strip all around and place it around the rim. Moisten with water and place the pastry over the casserole, pressing the edges firmly together, turning them up slightly. Make a hole in the crust to let the steam escape. Bake 30 minutes. Dissolve the gelatine in a little cold water and stir it into the remaining liquid. When the pie is removed from the oven, pour the gelatinized liquid through the hole. Cool and then refrigerate for at least 12 hours before serving. This will keep for days.

† SHEPHERD'S PIE

8 potatoes	4 cups cold roast beef or lamb, cubed
butter, milk, salt, and pepper	
1 cup chopped onion	4 cups thick gravy, left over or canned
	2 egg yolks

Peel and boil the potatoes until soft. Drain and put back on the stove for a moment to dry, shaking the pan to keep them from burning. Mash the potatoes and beat with 2 tbsp butter and enough hot milk to make a thick purée. Season well with salt and pepper.

Cook the chopped onion with 2 tbsp butter until soft. Spread a layer of the mashed potatoes in the bottom of a greased casserole. Cover with a layer of the cubed meat and gravy and sprinkle with some of the onion. Season with a little salt and pepper. Repeat the process once or twice depending on the size and shape of the casserole. Finish with a layer of mashed potato, marking it with the tines of a fork to resembly the top crust of a pastry pie. Brush with egg yolks, slight beaten. Bake 25 minutes at 400° F.

† VEAL KIDNEYS IN DIJON SAUCE

6 veal kidneys	½ cup dry white wine
4 tbsp butter	1 cup chicken bouillon
1 tbsp chopped onion	½ cup heavy cream
1 tbsp chopped parsley	2 tsp Dijon mustard
2 tbsp flour	freshly ground black pepper
	1 tbsp gelatine

Remove the film and fat from the kidneys and cut into cubes. Heat the butter and cook the kidneys for 3 minutes over high heat. Turn them, reduce the heat, and add the chopped onion and parsley. Cook 3 minutes longer, stirring frequently. Remove the kidneys from the pan with a slotted spoon. Stir the flour into the butter in the pan. Moisten with the white wine and bouillon and stir with a wooden spoon until well blended. Reduce the heat to very low and simmer 15 minutes. Add the cream, which has been blended with the mustard. Season to taste with salt and pepper. Reheat the kidneys in the sauce but do not boil. Serve on buttered toast.

† SAUTEED POTATO BALLS
(4 servings)

1½ lbs new potatoes	1 tbsp chopped chives
4 tbsp butter	1 tbsp chopped parsley
2 tbsp oil	salt and pepper

Cut balls from new potatoes with a small potato scoop. Dry the balls without washing them. You should have 3½ to 4 cups. Heat 2 tbsp butter with the oil in a large skillet. When very hot, sauté the potato balls 2 to 3 minutes. Shake the skillet to turn the potatoes over, and continue cooking until golden brown. Reduce the heat, cover, and continue cooking 15 minutes, shaking the pan frequently. They should be crispy outside and soft inside when tested with a knife.

Pour off the cooking fat, and add 2 tbsp butter, the chopped herbs, salt, and pepper. Shake over the heat just until the butter is melted and the potato balls coated. Other garden-fresh herbs—basil, tarragon, and dill—can be used deliciously with the potatoes.

† WILTED CUCUMBERS

3 cucumbers	6 tbsp peanut or olive oil
salt	⅛ tsp black pepper
2 tbsp tarragon vinegar	2 tsp chopped parsley

Peel the cucumbers unless they are freshly picked from the garden. Slice lengthwise in half and scoop out the seeds with a teaspoon. Slice thin and place the slices on a plate. Sprinkle liberally with salt and let stand for 30 to 40 minutes. Rinse thoroughly in cold water and dry on a clean dish towel, patting them dry to remove all excess water. Serve in a glass bowl with a sauce made of vinegar, oil, and pepper. More salt will not be necessary. Sprinkle with the chopped parsley.

† LENTIL SALAD

1 box (16 oz) dried lentils	2 cloves garlic
½ cup sliced onions	Vinaigrette Sauce (see page 259)
salt and pepper	chopped parsley

Soak the lentils overnight in cold water. Drain. Cover with water and add the onions, 1 tsp salt, and ¼ tsp black pepper. Cook over moderate heat until tender, about 45 minutes. Drain completely. Press the garlic over the beans and stir in the sauce. Place in a nonmetal bowl. Sprinkle chopped parsley over the top. Serve cold.

† APPLE AND BLACKBERRY TART

Dessert Pastry (page 260) ¼ tsp salt
2 cups blackberries   2 tbsp flour
4 tart apples   ¼ tsp nutmeg
½ cup sugar

Roll out the pastry ¼ inch thick and line a pie plate with it. Cut the remaining pastry into strips ¾ inch wide.

Pick over the berries and put them in a bowl. Peel, core, and slice the apples and mix with the berries. Combine the sugar, salt, flour, and nutmeg, and stir into the fruit very gently. Fill the pie shell with the mixture and cover with a lattice top made of the pastry strips, pressing the ends down firmly. An extra strip around the edge will help contain the juice. Place in a shallow pan to catch any juice that may run over, and bake 45 minutes at 425° F. Serve warm or cold with heavy cream or Cheddar cheese.

† SUMMER PUDDING

1 cup water   2 cups currants
¾ cup sugar   firm white bread
3 cups raspberries, blackberries,   butter
    or loganberries   cream

Boil the water and sugar for 3 minutes. Add the fruit, cover and simmer 5 minutes. Strain the juice and force the pulp through a fine sieve. Keep the pulp and juice separate. Line the bottom and sides of a buttered soufflé dish with ¼ inch slices of buttered bread from which the crusts have been cut away, making sure that the inner surfaces of the dish are completely covered. Spread a thick layer of the fruit pulp on the bottom, cover with another layer of bread and soak it with the juice. Repeat the process twice and finish with a layer of bread thoroughly soaked with juice. Put a plate with a pound weight in it on the top to press the pudding down, and chill for 12 hours in the refrigerator. Turn it out on a dessert plate and serve with heavy cream.

† TREACLE TART

1 cup all-purpose flour	2 tbsp ice water
½ tsp salt	½ lemon
1 tsp baking powder	4 tbsp golden syrup
3 tbsp vegetable shortening	4 tbsp soft bread crumbs
3 tbsp butter	

Combine the flour, salt, and baking powder in a bowl. With a single electric beater, a pastry blender, or two knives, cut the shortening and butter into the flour mixture until it is pebbly in texture. Add enough ice water to make the dough sticky so that it will form a ball. Let it rest at least 20 minutes. Roll it out ¼ inch thick and line an 8 inch shallow pie plate, trimming the edges neatly with a sharp knife. Cut the remaining pastry into thin strips.

Grate the lemon rind and squeeze out the juice. Mix the rind and juice with the syrup into the bread crumbs, and fill the pastry with the mixture, smoothing it with a knife. Crisscross the strips of pastry over the top of the filling to make a lattice. Turn the edge of the bottom crust over the ends of the strips and press down firmly all around. Bake at 425° F for 20 minutes. Serve hot or cold with sweetened whipped cream.

Murder
in the
Village

SIXTEEN

The Patchwork Quilt: The Prospect of Evil in Eden

The setting of a detective story . . . is of cardinal importance. The plot must appear to be an actual record of events springing from the terrain of its operations. . . . A familiarity with the terrain and a belief in its existence are what give the reader his feeling of ease and freedom in manipulating the factors of the plot to his own (which are also the author's) ends.

WILLARD HUNTINGTON WRIGHT,
"The Great Detective Stories"

Tranquillity was born in the English village. The hum of bees and the almost audible nodding of roses, the quiet nattering of little old ladies spinning their busy webs of gossip, as they go in and out of the shops on the High Street, the distant huffing of the train, are the lulling hum of life before the shriek.

It is a world entirely comprehensible, ritually ordered, completely trustworthy, where all the familiar pleasures reassemble themselves, symbols of security set out like the large crockery bowl, the flour tin, the well-worn wooden spoon that heralded an afternoon of baking in the sweet warm kitchen of childhood.

Were we to step down from a Green Line bus onto the High Street, we would immediately have our bearings. We recognize the street. It is so familiar we might have grown up there. At one end is the train station, the contact with the outer world; at the other, the church, the contact with the Other World; at a discreet distance, the very much this-world pub. For a stamp, we step briskly into the sweet shop. For a headache powder, we go into the chemist's shop. Up and down, on both sides of the street, are the small clusters of necessary shops and businesses nestled in the midst of Queen Anne and Georgian houses. There is the bank, the solicitor's offices, the estate agent's, the bakery with the still-warm loaves of currant bread and jars of homemade greengage jam in the window. The grocer's with its tins of biscuits, rennet powder, fish paste, golden syrup; the greengrocer's mounds of cox apples, bananas, pippins, potatoes, runner beans, oranges. The butcher's shop with blinds down for early closing. The antique shop, cluttered with Derbyshire figurines, china souvenirs of town fairs, cut-glass pitchers, and Georgian silver spoons. The tea shop window, offering pink cream cakes and sugary buns; small bunches of flowers on the tables, and an atmosphere of pastel gossip within.

Darting to and fro like bees collecting pollen or white butterflies about the cauliflower and cabbage plants are all the characters that Agatha Christie, number one town planner of mystery land, has made us believe. Busy, jolly ladies hurrying off to committee meetings at the vicarage to plan a fête, picking up a bit of fish for dinner, smiling abstractedly at a rosy-cheeked child, mailing a scarf to a niece for her birthday, nodding pleasantly at the tall, lean police constable, thinking of tansy tea for a sick friend, plotting the spring garden, settling for a moment in the tea shop, their parcels beside them, before setting off again, stopping at the lending library on the way home.

Of all the murder mystery settings, the village is perhaps the most ideal. It provides the formal setting for the irregular occurrence. Because of the limitation of its physical boundaries and the static quality of its social structure, nothing extraneous distracts us. It adheres best to Chesterton's view in "The Domesticity of the Detective," that ". . . the great detective story deals with small things."

Guests down for the weekend at the Great Hall, although physically more confined, are unknown quantities compared to the villagers. Within the confines of their social strata, the guests may act in any number of ways; their roles are not automatically assigned. On the continental train, again more physically limited than the village, the characters are even more diverse. Not only do they come from different countries, they come from different classes, a greater source of "foreignness" than mere difference of nationality.

It is essential to the tale of mystery in the village that the citizens not only live in close physical proximity but be—as it were—in each other's pockets. Spinsters must be nosy, maids gossip, fishmongers' boys carry news with the fish, and everyone be ferociously curious, so that the unknown factors in the mystery be gradually revealed—the daughters by earlier marriages, the anonymous letter scandal in another village, the hypochondria of the lawyer's wife. Every window must be an eye to the street that conceals the gimlet eye of the potential talebearer. As the vicar in Agatha Christie's *Murder at the Vicarage* comments ruefully, "It is a mystery to me . . . how anyone gets any nourishment in this place. They must eat their meals standing by the window so as to be sure of not missing anything."

The small, unexciting village, like Agatha Christie's St. Mary Mead, becomes the world in microcosm; a world no larger and little more complex than a patchwork quilt, here with gay flowers, there with bold shapes; and a sky spreading a canopy of homely philosophy overhead. The fixity of people, time, and place provides a screen across which the plot may move in swift contrast.

It is called England; in fact, it is not. The resemblance is largely physical: the green sward, the roads leading to London, the hedgerows, the heavy-leaved beeches, the spires. It is the world of the expected, where we are able to predict the events of five o'clock in the afternoon, as easily as we predict the sunrise. To know that the vicar will stop in the vestry to reprove the choirboys for sweet-sucking, the spinster pinch aside the lace curtains to spy up and down the lane, the Horsy Lady bark out an order to her brother, the colonel pause by the stream to speculate on the trout, and as each disappears, that another colonel, another Horsy Lady, another vicar will rise up like a mushroom in his or her place. The village proves the human rhythm as eternal as that of the crops or tide. The figures go through their rhythmic patterns, as on a large music box, turning, bowing, moving around the top to a tinkling tune. As Chesterton says in "A Defense of Detective Stories," ". . . we must give a fair credit to the popular literature which . . . declines to regard the present as prosaic or the common as commonplace." In the village's patchwork of ordinariness, the familiar becomes threatening, the humdrum exciting, when murder settles in.

The village is a stagnant pool, says her nephew but, says Miss Marple, a drop of water from that pool swarms with life. In St. Mary Mead it also swarms with death. The morality fable has been taken away from fairyland, the forces of evil—giants, goblins, dwarfs—given the faces of people we know, and they come closer to winning than they do in fairyland. The picture-postcard village is a place where nothing ever happens—except murder.

Then, the vicar, the colonel, the doctor, the spinsters, the chief constable, the familiar characters drop their trowels, come out from behind their hedges, and rush to the forum, the High Street, to share their gossip, and regard each other with sudden suspicion. While murder draws everyone into the arena with centrifugal force, acquaintance of a lifetime mysteriously becomes as naught. In an instant, all are ready to look at old actions for new meanings.

Whereas murder in the sylvan setting horrifies by its contrast with a beneficent nature, murder in the village shocks by contrasting the outrageous act of one with a benign mankind. Now the reaction is not how could a corpse lie hidden in a leafy copse or bludgeoned on the hearthrug, but how could that fluttery little lady lift an ax and slaughter her employer? Or how, as the colonel will say with a great deal of spluttering, can one suspect Derek, I've known him since he was a boy, we've watched him grow up or, I knew his mother. Derek is, in other words, a part of the charmed circle, the world of innocence. He knows the rules; that he should break the rules is unthinkable.

What we relied on, a trusted human being or type of human being, stands to betray us, to be not innocent, but the embodiment of evil. The threat is, after all, within the walls. It is not, as the chief constable in Margery Allingham's *The Estate of the Beckoning Lady* fondly believes, "Motorists. Terrible fellers from God knows where. Depend upon it, one of those has run down some poor feller, carted him for twenty miles or so, and then got rid of him." It is not an outsider. Could it even be ourselves?

Goblins invade the room, the benign porcelain figures spring into menacing postures, the tea kettle hisses, and the author cries, with Hercule Poirot, mistrust what you see: that lady who talks so much of her tea shop is a murderess; the very conventional doctor is a murderer; that silly young man with a monocle, the ridiculous little foreigner with the egg-shaped head are master detectives; the gently flowing stream harbors a body. Everyone and everything is hiding something. Nothing is what it seems, there is a prospect of evil in Eden.

SEVENTEEN

Map-Making:
The Path of Evil

I fled Him, down the nights and down the days;
  I fled Him, down the arches of the years;
I fled Him, down the labyrinthine ways
  Of my own mind; and in the mist of running tears
I hid from Him, and under running laughter.
      Up vista-ed hopes I sped;
      And shot, precipitated,
Adown Titanic glooms of chasmed fears,
    From those strong Feet that followed, followed after.
      But with unhurrying chase,
      And unperturbéd pace,
    Deliberate speed, majestic instancy,
      They beat—and a Voice beat
      More instant than the Feet—
"All things betray thee, who betrayest Me."
              FRANCIS THOMPSON, *"The Hound of Heaven"*

A book with maps tucked within, either as endpapers or illustrations, should be pulled immediately from the library shelf, secreted under the arm, and rushed upstairs to a place on the night table under the bedside lamp, beside the traveling clock. It is bound to be good.

Maps indicate secret passageways. The relationship of the positions of the bedrooms. The path through the garden, past the pavilion, and into the woods. The desk in the library where the victim's head was found lolling on the desk. The flower pot where the gun was secreted. The door from the billiard room into the conservatory, and the well where the victim's body was, perhaps, meant to be dropped.

The map is an offer by the author to take us into the secret dwelling places of her mind, to make us believe we are active participants in the case. We are, in effect, taken in on the ground floor. We will know, she is saying, all that is known of the terrain. We will know the house, the grounds, the country, the lane like the back of our hands. Through the map, we are on the spot, immersed even more than by description in the locale, for a map, by being spatial, requires us to use our muscles. We climb the stairs, find our way to the boxroom, move aside the coats in the cloakroom, avoid the chest in the hall, feel the banisters beneath our hands.

As with the descriptions of food, the timetables, the self-conscious references by the author to "detective stories"—as if, in contrast, this were real—a map builds up the case for actuality. It is further evidence that the story is no story; this is not make-believe, this is true, this does exist; here is the place where it happened. The map proves the event and the place exist; and that we can get there.

It is essential for us to do so. For the map in the mystery is the visible plan of vengeance. It represents, in physical terms, the hunt through space, the implacable pursuit of the Hound of Heaven, pursuit made concrete. Through the map, the vast reaches of guilt are scaled down to human dimensions. By both illuminating and confining the search, the map makes possible solution or resolution. It proves, like the fixed moment, the existence of The Place, the specificness of guilt. By enclosing guilt, it proves guilt has its limits. By externalizing it, the map promises freedom from our own complicity.

The map in the mystery, unlike the map of the treasure hunt, the Lost Atlantis, the Fountain of Youth, or a New World with their hopes and joyous expectation, and reward waiting at the end, acknowledges the Fall. Those maps lead us directly back, return us to a state of innocence before guilt, and the admission, with evil, of death into the garden. In all those places, simply by arriving, locating the place, we will reattain innocence, and with it, eternal life.

Their search is only for The Place or The Good; the mystery search is for the Evil One, the Fallen Angel, for only with his discovery can we return to the good. The murder mystery map takes us past guilt, and requires a punishment. We, with society, seek like hunting dogs the track of the murderer who took away innocence—where he was at the hour of death, where he stood, what steps he took, by what means he entered, how the citadel was vulnerable. The map is, like the clues, the physical means by which we establish the murderer's guilt. The end is the cry, "Now, I have you. You cannot get away!"; the physical entrapment.

We follow the trail backward from the moment of the loss of innocence to what preceded it. Here he walked through the door, there he climbed over the wall. By means of the map, slowly, methodically, as we might tear a vine from the wall, we seek the source and root out evil, following the creepers of the weed to the central root beneath the ground, which is Hades or Death. For unless we can find the point of origin, the root, we cannot hope to remove evil. At the point when we find death poised with life, when the murderer raised his knife or gun into the air and aimed, we have located the moment of balance between innocence and guilt. Before that moment, there was no evil; after that moment, we were all involved. Finding that moment, and removing the perpetrator, who shifted the balance to guilt and death, we may return once more to the state of innocence, before we knew death. Locating and expunging evil, we free ourselves, for a moment, from guilt.

EIGHTEEN

The Constabulary: A-Hunting We Will Go

The Superintendent's expression was packed with semi-secret entertainment. . . . "Well sir, we've got the nasty thing right out of the way for you. There'll be a few fellows down there taking pictures and scraping up little bits of nonsense for a little while yet, but it'll be all tidy in no time. Not a bit of paper left on the grass."

MARGERY ALLINGHAM, *The Estate of the Beckoning Lady*

The police station is a red-brick building, ugly and of sound appearance. It is located at the end of the High Street; therefore, it is convenient, but not obtrusive. Within the station is one big, drab room behind a counter with an upright telephone. Behind the counter are several weathered desks with big typewriters for typing up reports on lost dogs, obscene phone calls, anonymous letters, etc. Seated here and there about the room is a sprinkling of constables, and a sergeant. The inspector is out, and the chief constable does not come in on a regular basis. There is the sound of a typewriter as a sergeant fills out a report on a lost dog, low conversation, the occasional jingle of the telephone, and the door opening on a constable carrying coffee in from the nearby pub.

County constabularies are not ordinarily hives of activity, but they are very game about picking up on a murder when one falls in their manor. Even so, the inspector is all manners and welcome when it turns out that a famous London policeman or idling detective just happens to be on holiday in the area, or visiting at the house where the murder took place. Thus ensues a gavotte of demurs. "No, I really mustn't. Just down on holiday, er—technically—don't you know." Modest blushes and stammers, followed by flatterings and urgings on the part of the local talent, who plead happiness at having the big bug on deck and long to be shown how, as it were. These little pleasantries accomplished, the big bug takes over everything, including the local light, who becomes his willing minion, and his staff, whom he presses into service, giving suggestions—cryptically delivered, so as not to tip his hand to the reader—where they might look, and how they might handle it. Friction does not exist, and they might have been operating as a team all their lives. Such is the selflessness and devotion of the police in their duty.

The prime functions of a policeman are to come to the front door, frighten the maid, wait in the library and deliver a warning, called "the customary warning," which suggests that from this moment forward everything you say will be taken down and may, at a later date, be used against you. People always continue talking, however.

Policemen arrive in packs after a crime. If the body has been found in field or ditch, they scour the area, pulling threads from twigs and stuffing them in bags, gathering up bits of rubbish, making casts of tire tracks. If it is an inside job, flashes flare as the photographer photographs every aspect of corpse and room, while the air fills with powder as they dust for fingerprints, and haul away scraps of dinner to be chemically analyzed. In the house, the police seal off rooms and work behind closed doors with a sergeant on duty at the door around the clock. Despite their occupation, the police are hard-working and relatively unobtrusive till they hit the kitchen where they create sociological problems the minute they swing open the baize door.

The chief constable of the county is a different kettle of fish from a constable, and they are not to be confused. A constable is simply a tall, taciturn but friendly young man who wears a bobby's helmet and carries a big stick. The county constable is a big pot. His job is important, and his ancestry is good. He is gentry, a member of an old county family, therefore inclined, when dealing with young men who are really too well brought up to murder and should, in any case, know better, to call them "my dear boy," and be ever so patient with their foibles. If such a young man should confess, the colonel—for he is sure to be an old army man—will call him a "damned young fool," and refuse to accept it. (It is always nice to be well-born in a mystery; the ranks, even if they are police, will close around you.) If the chief constable thinks the young man *has* done it, he will call him inconsiderate of others for perpetrating the crime.

The chief constable has great difficulty considering the prospect of more than one suspect, and two confessions will unsettle him completely. Chief constables are not known for flexibility. Chief constables have inspectors who are a whole other class. They frequently do not see eye to eye.

One of the village entertainments the chief constable provides, which will compete with a fête for numbers in attendance, is the inquest. Inquests bring out all the known facts, and surviving characters. It is a pause to sum up the facts of the crime to this point, so that both reader and author can start at "go" and see who gets to the solution first. If the author is good, the reader won't. In villages, the inquest is held at the local inn by the chief constable and the coroner. They establish whether or not a crime has been committed, and whether "by person or persons unknown," and the probable time and means. (Blunt instruments always go down well.) Everybody gets his say, and the villagers enjoy the event very much. It's always simply ages since the last one.

Chief constables snort because they are colonels. All colonels snort and say, "Quite," "Gad," and "Shocking." They have keen, gooseberry eyes, blue, of course, and bushy eyebrows. All colonels have mustaches on which to chew in emergencies. They are liable to know the district more in terms of hunting than any legal or extralegal recollections. Therefore, if you wish to draw attention to the location of the body in a ditch, it is best to point out that it is the one that is full of birds in the winter. The chief constable will alert immediately. Not about the murder (which he will already have forgotten), but the recollection of the game.

NINETEEN

The Vicar: Heavenly Daze

"But as dear Miss Marple says, you are so unworldly, dear Vicar."

AGATHA CHRISTIE, *Murder at the Vicarage*

Vicars are sweet. For one thing, they are addled. There is only one person surer to be more addled than a professor, and that is a vicar. It's all that spirituality. When you're in constant touch with the On High, it shows up below. It is difficult to manage the simplest things. Like separating quarreling matrons, controlling a recalcitrant housekeeper, knowing you're not hungry because you've already eaten. Or remembering where you should be. At his most addled, the vicar, sitting in the chancel, cannot remember whether he has not yet begun or has already preached his sermon.

The vicar is always in his study writing boring, erudite sermons through which the parishioners will nod the following Sunday, when he's not out boring them in the evening with dull, Latin-spattered conversation. As he writes on the theme "Does the Greek spelling of Caiaphus indicate he was actually Dionysius in disguise?" his abstraction will be such that he barely raises his head to notice a parishioner frantically capering through the peonies on his way to the police station, or falling over, tangled in the periwinkles. It is a prime rule of conduct when setting off for police stations to travel over obscure little footpaths that pass through people's gardens until you come to the vicarage stile, which must be leaped over in order to pass through the gate and beyond. Even if the vicar does look up, he won't see because he has mislaid his glasses on top of his head or, if they're on, they've only made him more short-sighted.

The vicar's study must be crammed with tomes, and be disorderly. It must give on the garden, because they all do, and so that the vicar, gazing out in his short-sighted haze, can behold the lilies of the field, and gain inspiration for the sermon he is in process of composing.

A dog lying on the hearth never hurt anything but, of course, the dog may have other ideas. He will be better off on the hearth of a country gentleman who appreciates, and never forgets him. Vicars are really too addled for dogs. And a dog likes an occasional outing, so that he can hold his tail up with his peers. To spend a whole season without going on a shoot can put you down. When the vicar goes out, he will head—if he can remember long enough—toward the home of a sick parishioner. He will turn up at the wrong house and give consolation for the wrong ailment, but never mind. The family can save it for the next time. No life for a dog.

Not remembering where he is going is just one of the vicar's problems. It can be even worse, if he remembers. Then, he must carry out one of his temporal duties, a little spiritual prying, always a loathsome task for shy men, which vicars are. This will cause him to mop his brow in the shade of the tulip tree, and take the long way round the lily pond in order to delay joining the family on the lawn. If he encounters an alien spirit in the atmosphere, he will make pious observations and debate whether to suggest prayer, a serious and improving book, a tennis party, or an informal dance. If, however, the vicar seems to be getting a purchase on the fleece of one of his flock, he may perk up a little. It will quite improve his appetite for tea, so that he may need a second slice of seed cake. Sometimes, in his study, the vicar gets strange cravings for this or that parishioner to have a deeper spiritual experience, but fortunately that is quickly routed by another of the housekeeper's failures in the kitchen. Spiritual experiences cannot make much headway against the raucous fumes of a pudding boiling dry.

Still, everybody loves the vicar, who is rather like a faded old rose, and they turn to him with all their problems—about mating their dogs, not about murder. Even so, the vicar may encounter Something. He, too, may tangle his feet on the garden path, and it won't be in periwinkles.

The moral tone of vicars is such that people feel compelled to apologize after saying "damn." Further indications of their spiritual condition is given by their having names such as "Harmon(y)," "Greengrave," and "Clement," lest we fail to get the idea. However, vicars themselves regard tendencies to mysticism, fasting, or any other signs of overzealous religiosity with as much suspicion as any member of their parish. Accordingly, should any such tendencies appear in their curates, the vicar attempts to defeather their religious flights forthwith, and bring them down to earth. In Margery Allingham's *The Estate of the Beckoning Lady* the vicar remarks, ". . . you can be as pi as you like privately, but you mustn't think too much about it or you may forget yourself and mention it," which is to say that "a Christian gentleman must never run the risk of degenerating into a vulgar Christian."

Ineffectual vicars are the nice compromise the English have effected between the feeling that they really ought to have a church, and the deep suspicion of the religious. Like having a declawed cat.

TWENTY

The Spinster:
The Town Conscience

"... Aunt Emily ticked me off good and proper. She inti-
mated that she was under no illusions as to why her affectionate family had gathered round her! And she also inti-
mated that the said affectionate family would be disap-
pointed. Nothing being handed out but affection—and not
so much of that."

AGATHA CHRISTIE, *Poirot Loses a Client*

One sure sign of the spinster is the letter she writes. A spinster
can be recognized from an envelope held at a distance of five
feet. Her handwriting is described as spidery, i.e., as if a spider
has dunked itself in an inkpot and then set off busily back and
forth across the page. The ink is probably purple to match the
scent of lavender in the air, and the impassioned tone. The spinster's letter is as full as her speech of exclamations, hints, and

underlined words. If, when the letter is finished, her writing is still legible, she writes across her letter to save paper, thus insuring a total want of communication.

There is no one so pure as a spinster, which may explain her overexcited way of speaking, a kind of verbal blushing. It takes very little indeed to open up the shock valves. But it is *so* stimulating to do so, she will have her ear against the wall all day long, just in case.

In a mystery, this nosiness is all to the good, and it is a clever man who takes advantage of it. When murder strikes a village, the first person a policeman should contact is the spinster—a gold mine of everybody's business. If a murder takes place in another village, the spinster may be sent in by the detective, much as a canary might be sent into a coal mine with a gas leak, to snuffle out every secret in miles by gossiping, collecting subscriptions for charitable causes, and drinking tea. Spinsters have stout kidneys. A spinster moves into a respectable boardinghouse, poses as a potential resident of the town, and lets nature take its course. Boardinghouse landladies enjoy nothing better than a good chat to a sympathetic spinster.

The spinster is an expert on anything she touches: gardening, housekeeping, nursing, life. She has very strong ideas. Her cupboards are filled with home remedies and brews made from her grandmother's receipts. This expertise and rightness makes the spinster a little less popular than she should be with the fuzzier-edged members of the village, who would rather not be reminded of right and wrong.

When nephews or nieces get into financial scrapes, a really strong elderly spinster will let them bail themselves out, even though her mattress is lumpy with gold. She will sleep well anyway; she wouldn't dream of not doing so. Treatment of this sort for her relatives is good for the character. One of them, who is more interested in a good horse than a good character, may insure a good long rest for her. However, unlike femmes fatales or maids, who seem only capable of being killed, a spinster can be victim, murderess, or detective, and excel at whatever her choice.

Given ordinary circumstances, a spinster would never die. She is made up of iron, whalebone, and will, which she dresses up with black lace shawls—tossed over her person like antimacassars—caps, and even mittens. Her caps make it difficult at times to tell whether she's dead or alive if she's in bed, or if she's been exchanged, like Red Riding Hood's grandmother, for the murderer.

The spinster puts down suggestions for sleeping draughts (which is very hard on would-be murderers) as too soft. She is pretty steady on her pins, though not above a topple down the stairs, if pushed, or in the street, if in a hurry. From either, she emerges only lightly bruised, though the former occurrence will make her change her will. She can be cured of the most serious ailments with beef tea, brandy, and a hot water bottle. When in bed, however, she is even more crochety than other invalids, except old men, because she is so full of spunk.

One of the most useful characteristics of a spinster as a victim is her age. Age, in a victim, is a very useful attribute. Even with the spirited, it can't help but make murder easier. But more important, it allows the author to make the spinster attractive enough so that we can become a little bit fond of the old bird, and yet not suffer enormously when she's done in. Thus, the problem of making the victim unsympathetic so that we don't grieve when she dies is avoided. People simply expect old ladies to die, one way or another, and are more inclined to write it off than if the victim is young. It's like starting a hare. They are expendable.

Spinsters enjoy a good battle with anybody. They often take on their doctors who, with the same remarkable longevity as lawyers, have seen them through all their illnesses since childhood. They combat the doctor in a friendly way. They combat their companions with more venom. It is good for their circulation. It makes a focus for the day. The bedridden spinster spends much of her time putting down, teasing, and outfoxing the poor-spirited, dull-witted companion and then embarrassing her pink by mentioning that she appreciates her. Old ladies adore sending their companions on wild-goose chases, so that they can get into mischief; or to the lending library, so that they can complain about their book choices.

When she is on her feet, the spinster attends church, and means it. Fasts before Easter services, and is a lot harder on heaven and earth than the vicar. She does not involve herself in mush-headed good works the way the Horsy Lady will. She lets the poor stay that way. Poverty is good for the soul. She has moral fiber, and we all know what that is. Spinsters are a social necessity. A spinster has the conscience that nobody else wants, but feels someone should have.

TWENTY-ONE

Miss Marple: Expert on Evil

"You surprise me," said Sir Henry Clithering. The ex-Commissioner of Scotland Yard turned to Miss Marple. "I always understood . . . that St. Mary Mead is a positive hotbed of crime and vice."

"Oh, Sir Henry!" protested Miss Marple, a spot of colour coming into her cheeks. "I'm sure I never said anything of the kind. The only thing I ever said was that human nature is much the same in a village as anywhere else, only one has opportunities and leisure for seeing it at closer quarters."

AGATHA CHRISTIE, "The Companion"

If one were ill, the nice kind of ill that is little more than a return to childhood cosseting and counterpanes, to glasses of hot lemonade and spoonfuls of honey meant to soothe away the last weakness of a fever, what could be more delicious than a visit from Miss Marple? To hear her light footsteps coming up the stairs—a fairy godmother, bringing homemade madeira jelly or medlar jam—settling herself for a gossip in the chair by the bed, there would be nothing more to do than sigh contentedly, and snuggle deeper in the covers.

In Miss Marple's hands, we are all children. A Peter Pan act of faith, and she is there, tidying the world to the dimensions of a patchwork quilt. Sorrow can be cured by elderberry wine. Murder is a game to tease away the boredom of invalidery. The sin of murder is somehow equivalent to the mischief of a favorite nephew, or of young Robbie—poor Robbie, since dead—who became Bishop of Westchester. Leaving a body in a stranger's library is a child's prank similar to Tommy Tidbit's putting a frog in the teacher's clock because he felt picked on. Evil itself, on which she is said to be an expert, is little worse than naughtiness; as predictable, as understandable. Yet, if she believes the worst, gives no one the benefit of the doubt, and has never seen any reason to regret it, it is without a sense of reproach. For all its prevalence, evil fails to depress her, nor has she any misguided urge to combat it. Evil is here to stay, and rather a good thing, too. Like a beneficent Mme. Defarge, Miss Marple sits in its shadow, spinning fleecy white wool imperturbably through her arthritic fingers. She may observe it, sigh a little over it, and participate agreeably in its resolution without dropping a stitch. The only effect it has is to energize her forces, bring a twinkle to her eye, and pink spots to her cheeks.

Her nephew Raymond West lays the origin of her knowledge of evil to her Victorian upbringing, holding the common viewpoint that beneath those benevolent exteriors were minds like sinks. Miss Marple says the Victorians simply knew a lot about human nature. Even without such a salutary education, Miss Marple would have had the benefit of the narrowed focus that comes of living in a rural village, where no action is lost to one's neighbor's eyes, or tongue. When Raymond sends modern novels for her enlightenment, Miss Marple is only astonished at their innocence.

Miss Marple resolves crime by one rule: that life is little more than a series of resemblances; there are a certain number of patterns of human behavior, and they repeat. Having recognized a pattern, one can foresee the outcome. Two situations with no external likeness can involve the same set of feelings. It would make perfectly good sense, for example, when speculating on the behavior of two politicians who fell out in a smoke-filled room, to say that that reminds me of the time Aunt Ida spilled the iced watermelon juice on Cousin Lucy's dog. It's simply easier if you are a little old lady who takes rests in the afternoon and wears gray lace for dinner in a Caribbean nightclub.

While the village flurries, and the police plod, Miss Marple patters along, playing a close hand. She reads devotional books on waking, breakfasts in bed, supervises her maid, struggles with the gardener, serves on committees for orphanages, buys presents for her great-nephews, goes to jumble sales, and worries about the fall in popularity of hybrid tea roses. She plays, for everyone's benefit, super-aunt. Settling on terrace, veranda, or by the fire, she employs her "one weapon, conversation" to good effect, never offended if her innocent babbling is mistaken for senility, as she fills up her stores of gossip. All of this, plus her parallels and pithy observations, are sandwiched between tea and biscuits; indulged in without embarrassment, as the prerogative of little old ladies who must, after all, be put up with.

In common with Hercule Poirot, when alert for a solution, Miss Marple is undistractable. She keeps a steady eye on the probable and, in case of emergency, never believes anyone at all. Though properly gentle and demure, she is as bold and unscrupulous in action as he, and not averse to the occasional dainty lie, and healthy doses of eavesdropping. However, she has the good grace to blush and dissemble. She does love her garden, and bird watching is so interesting, you know. What luck that the garden makes such a good post to spy from, and that the same binoculars used for bird watching can give you a marvelous view down the road. And should the chat coming from the lane tickle her fancy, she has only to drop to her knees and rootle around in the weeds to salve her conscience.

Even at the dénouement, she continues to play her role; while explaining the reasoning that brought her to the solution, she wanders off the subject much as one might forget her stitches. Exposé finished, there is simply a sense of knitting being gathered up and put in its bag as, without further ado, Miss Marple steps briskly out to the kitchen to check on the progress of a flan in the oven. And we, having been amused and provoked, on an afternoon of malaise, may drop off to sleep, knowing we will wake to a well-managed world, where flans bake in the oven and fill the air with sweetness, and man's worst crime can be tamed by a little old lady.

TWENTY-TWO

Companions: The Art of Living

"Companions don't play tennis or golf. They might possibly play golf-croquet, but I have always understood that they wind wool and wash dogs most of the day."

AGATHA CHRISTIE, *The Mystery of the Blue Train*

Companions are nothing but Kleenex cases. Whereas maids only sniffle in extremity—when the police come, and after a really good funeral—companions are at it pretty much of the time. They have their feelings, you know. And there is no one an aged, infirm employer enjoys abusing more.

Trained for nothing at all, they irritate the sick, and speed the dying. It might be worthwhile to hire them for that reason alone, if the outcome were a bit surer. They annoy with over-helpfulness and general silliness, following the doctor's orders to the letter, continually coming in with egg dishes and using "we" like the worst nurses, which drives the invalid-employer mad.

However, there are a few things companions can do. They can pick up dropped stitches in knitting; they can prepare a proper breakfast of tea made with boiling water, eggs boiled exactly three-and-three-quarter minutes, evenly browned toast, a nice pat of butter and a small jar of honey, as Miss Marple attests in *The Mirror Crack'd.*

If Kleenex obscures the companion's face, she can also be recognized by the books she carries, her Balbriggan stockings, the velvet work bag of knitting wools she takes up to her employer's bedroom at night, and a tendency to indulge in spiritualism and food fads. The biggest treat a companion can think of is to nip off for a séance, or have a couple of spiritually minded friends in to tea.

The abuse a companion takes she repays as best she can by seeing to it she gets a whack at the lolly. Also by blushing painfully, her pince-nez awry, and mumbling that, after all, she has her feelings. And by snooping. If you ever open a door suddenly, a spinster, a companion, and Hercule Poirot are almost sure to topple through. The companion will automatically land at the bottom of the heap. She is such a poor lot, there is nothing for it but to refer to her as "a person." The only other group so often accorded this treatment is the police.

Doors with keyholes, or simple cracks, act like magnets for companions. Even her employer will not know her business as well as the companion. There is always a tray to be brought into the room, when the solicitor has come to call, and one can stand on one foot, and then the other, indefinitely, when it's a matter of delaying an entrance in order to overhear something.

When the companion takes up spiritualism, there is always the possibility of fraud. Through her, by her, of her. Fraud means a medium with beads, and hennaed hair. All kinds of hints and warnings can be thrown out by the medium to the weak, receptive mind (the companion's). Mediums are in constant radio contact with the Dear Ones, who have Passed Over. No matter how remarkable the changes—from irascible to sweet, from tall to short, or vice versa—the Dear Ones are still, somehow recognizably, the Dear Ones. Dim spinsters make excellent subjects for Dear Ones, who are invariably lost loves their mothers wouldn't let them marry because they weren't good enough. Or the mothers themselves. No rest for the wicked. Dear Ones can suggest any number of things: that one would be happier playing out there with them, or some relevant change in a will.

The companion will eat it up with a spoon. To the hilarity of her employer, who will see it as yet another opportunity for a round of cat-and-mouse. Until the tables are turned, and the companion, with a little help from her friends, flings down her work bag, does a little something to her employer's soup, and rolls off in the Rolls to the hairdresser. Never put the wind up a spirit.

TWENTY-THREE

Tempest in a Teapot: The Care and Brewing of Tea

"... I'm feeling better already, Miss Climpson, fitter and brighter in every way. Either I'm getting a line on the thing, or else it's your tea. That's a good, stout-looking pot. Has it got any more in it?"

"Yes, indeed," said Miss Climpson, eagerly. "My dear father used to say I was a great hand at getting the *utmost* out of a tea pot. The secret is to *fill* up as you *go* and never empty the pot completely."

DOROTHY L. SAYERS, *Strong Poison*

To brew the best tea, it is as necessary to have a spinster as it is to have a virgin for a truffle hunt. Only a spinster can provide that atmosphere of coziness, knickknackery, and chintz so important to the taste. Tea is made, of course, by first installing a hob on which to hang the kettle, then scattering antimacassars liberally about the room, and finding the cat. A collection of small flower pots with African violets is helpful, but not essential.

The ultimate tribute to the teapot, its temple, the tea shop, and its vestal virgin, the spinster, was paid by Agatha Christie in *Funerals Are Fatal.* The genteel companion, Miss Gilchrist, kills her employer with a hatchet all for the love of a tea shop. Instead of a faded picture of an old beau on her bedroom wall (ready to be brought into service should a séance arise), there is a photograph of a tea shop she once had, called The Willow-Tree. A victim of the war. Like a mother with a very special child, she babbles about the blue willow-patterned china, or the jam and scones she used to prepare, or trade secrets for making brioches and chocolate éclairs. She is more often seen with flour on her hands than blood. Miss Gilchrist's obsession for the return to gentility a tea shop would afford is so great she kills for a pittance, and is taken away to the meting out of justice, happily planning the curtains.

So much tea is poured in a mystery, one comes away a bit squelchy after reading. So many sweet biscuits are served one could build a hundred Hansel-and-Gretel houses. Tea is the great restorer. It seeps into the nooks and crannies of the soul. It is oil on troubled waters. It is applied, like a hot compress wherever it hurts, with a faith and fervor that could only be bred in a conscientiously, securely, puritanically Protestant country such as England. Prayer is for Papists; whisky, for shock.

There is something crisping about tea. None of the florid, suspect luxury of coffee. Tea cries out to stiffen the lip, and be on with it. Tea quenches tears and thirst. It is an opening for the pouring out of troubles. It eases shyness, and lubricates gossip. While it is not in itself sympathetic, in the right hands tea acts as a backing force to tender ministrations. The mighty to the lowly assuage with tea, cure for body and soul.

Tea pours with equal grace from glazed brown pots or vast cauldrons of furbelowed silver. It washes through kitchens, where the lino cracks and the housewife offers a cuppa char, or slips, a perfect amber arch, into gold-stippled cups on the lawn of a stately home—its crystalline, chuckling voice covering any awkward moments with delicacy.

There are proper teas and, perhaps, improper teas, high teas and low. A proper tea is offered by an overbustly, oversolicitous matron who feels you look peaked and in need of immediate sustenance. A proper tea should, therefore, be substantial: Marmite, eggs, meat pies, sandwiches, cake, the lot. The substance of a proper tea is not actually different from high tea, which has stood in place of supper for hundreds of years for thousands of English schoolchildren. To be truly British, tea should be imbalanced in favor of carbohydrates—therefore, bread-and-butter sandwiches, plus sandwiches (kept nicely moist beneath a dampened napkin), fruitcake, and cakes.

Tea is best brewed in the brown pot. Otherwise, any china pot. The pot is "hotted up" with boiling water, which is allowed to sit for a moment before it is tossed out with an air. A teaspoonful of tea added for each cup, and one for the pot. The water for tea is of such moment, gentlemen traveling abroad often require special spring waters lest they encounter a foreign admixture to their favorite bouquet. The water must not boil a moment beyond its open, rolling bubble or the mineral content becomes proportionately higher. The brew then steeps for three to five minutes. Certain teas grow bitter if left longer, so second pots may have to be prepared for second cups. If tea is too strong, water will thin it, but not reduce the bitterness. Tea can be as deep and opaque as coffee or very little darker than water. In order that the flow never falter, a jug of hot water should stand by the smaller jug of warmed milk and the sugar bowl (no lumps, please).

Because England is inclined to be damp and chilly, and the houses drafty, the teapot may—though this is common—be given a little coat of its own, called a cozy, to wear to the table. A tea cozy is floral and quilted chintz, or a lumpish, unrecognizable crocheted affair made by an abysmal aunt. Some pots are further accoutered with tiny, tea-stained sponges attached to their nozzles to prevent drips.

The container in which the tea is stored is an understandably regal affair of antique Indian brass, lead-lined wood, or exotically devised porcelain, and is called a caddy. When the tea is a swirling maelstrom ready to be served, a strainer is placed over the cup to be sure the tea is clear. The strainer, as is proper with ceremonial vessels has, in turn, its own resting place above a little stand, or hooked over the slop bowl. Despite the revolting name, a slop bowl is a superbly proportioned, exquisitely decorated piece of china. To add the final, mystical note to the ceremony, a silver bell may stand on the tea table with which to ring for the servants for more cake, more milk, more hot water, or the police.

Tea kettles, apart from making tea, hot water for bottles, and singing, are very important utensils in a mystery if you haven't a letter opener, and wouldn't use one if you had. To unstick an envelope, you send whoever else is in the kitchen out of it. Be sure not to arouse suspicions, or they may dash back in and surprise you.

When the room is empty (check behind the fridge and stove to be sure), fill up the kettle. Put the kettle on the fire. Bring to a boil. Be sure to wait for a steady jet of steam. This will be about seven minutes for an average kettle. Keep an ear cocked. Hold envelope over steam. Slip knife under flap. Pry open very gently. Pull out contents, and read will, letter, or shopping list. If latter, scan for hidden meanings. If interrupted, slide knife into garter, and hide envelope behind stove, being sure to fold the flap backward to prevent resealing.

Make tea with leftover water.

Sometimes, spinsters get tired of their High Street shopping-and-tea-after routine, and take the cheap Thursday train to

London for the sales, and to switch suitcases and catch murderers at the station's Left Luggage. After her adventures, the spinster may choose to refresh herself by having tea in the lounge hall of a hotel, or take it on the return train.

Tea on the move may be the best tea of all. Served on British Railways, it is a rush and clatter of dishes which jump up and down—apparently from the excitement of travel—all the way from London to Plymouth, and back again, if they're not required. In the dim light of declining afternoon and three-watt bulbs, the crockery sits at empty tables in a state of eternal preparedness, as if endlessly waiting a macabre Mad Hatter's Tea Party—passengers advancing, eating, from table to table as the train runs along. The sandwiches—small circlings of tomatoes, sliced hard-boiled eggs, or fish paste on limp white bread, its crusts resolutely removed for refinement, and swathed in mayonnaise—contribute their own lifeless air, faintly enlivened by a tossing of mustard cress, and augmented by downtrodden, but resilient fruitcake. Thus, the bottom-heavy tradition of starchy foods at teatime is upheld, even in transit.

The civilizing effects of tea, perhaps more than the building of roads, or even the drinking of gin, has been one of the largest contributions England made to civilizing her empire. For centuries, wherever the flag waved, it was an amiable way for people to gather together under pith helmets or parasols for a well-mannered chat, to push sweet morsels in their mouths, and forget the ruddy natives hiding in the bush.

TWENTY-FOUR

The Omnipresent Omelet and the Immortal Sole

"The final course was a sweet omelette, which was made at the table in a chafing-dish by Philip Boyes himself. Both Mr. Urquhart and his cousin were very particular about eating an omelette the moment it came from the pan—and a very good rule it is, and I advise you all to treat omelettes in the same way and never allow them to stand, or they will get tough."

DOROTHY L. SAYERS, *Strong Poison*

It would be a mistake to assert that English mysteries continually proffer banquets of gourmet delights, succulent with rare delicacies, drawing on the cuisines of the world, imaginative and varied. Mushroom and chicken soups are very frequently eaten; the favorite dessert is apple tart. In fact, four or five dishes readily outnumber all the rest. For every pheasant served, there are six beefsteak and kidney puddings, for every lobster pilaf with raw medlars, there are three mixed grills. All mysteries are tributes to the English fondness for puddings whether as cup custard or a castle pudding with blackberry sauce. The island geography is clear from the prevalence of fish. The imperial past speaks through curries and chutneys.

No meal, save tea, is more often given its due than breakfast. But though aristocratic detectives seem as liable as any continental to begin their day luxuriating under the covers, the air redolent with coffee and croissants, England is clearly a country where hearty breakfasts send you porridged into the gray and foggy day.

For the principal meals, gammon, ham, veal, beef, and the traditional legs or saddles of mutton may be happily anticipated. On shooting, fishing and murdering holidays in Scotland and Ireland, the menu broadens to include pheasant, grouse, partridge, ducks, trout and salmon. But most meals rest on the world's most perfect sphere, the egg. Over fifty per cent of the time in a mystery, when a fork is poised, it is above an omelet.

Omelets have the advantage of gentleness of disposition, receptiveness to infinite variations, a speed of preparation that can put a dinner on the table in twenty minutes, and an adaptability that makes them an equal success at breakfast, lunch, or dinner, plus dessert. At any time refrigerators can be counted on to have eggs, butter and cream, which is to say, they always have an omelet in them. The only other things one needs are salt, a whisk, a small frying pan, a good wrist, and the culinary instructions of Sir Impey Biggs as they appear in Dorothy Sayers's *Strong Poison* (see above). Any little extras—mushrooms, herbs, onions, cheese, sour cream, caviar, potatoes, ham, jam—are all to the good; anything in the refrigerator that is the least bit feasible, and otherwise ill-fated. The pinnacle of the dessert omelet's murderous career is, of course, in the above-mentioned *Strong Poison* where, with a touch of arsenic, it does the job all by itself.

If the English mystery menu is puffed with omelets, saturated by tea, the *plat du* almost every *jour* is sole. One explanation is its quality. Dover sole, fresh from the Channel, is considered the best in the world. According to the housekeeper of the absent-minded canon in Agatha Christie's *At Bertram's Hotel*, "The advantages attached to a good Dover sole [are] manifold. It need not be introduced to the grill or frying pan . . . [but] . . . could be kept until the next day" should the canon forget where he was going and fail to turn up. Like the omelet, sole's ease and speed of preparation in sending the characters on their murderous ways is in its favor. The presentation of sole might also represent a belated concern on the author's part for the tattered nerves and jumpy stomachs of her characters who have, after all, been through a lot. Most simply, however, mystery writers probably like sole: it is an excellent fish, moist, tender, offensive to almost none, presentable in a thousand alluring ways. Sole, like chicken, by its very innocuousness accepts any number of blandishments—sauces, herbs, green grapes, the golden crispness of almonds, the sinuous trickle of butter—to appear and reappear on plate after plate before suspect after suspect in all sorts of homes after all sorts of crimes—the soul of the occasion.

TWENTY-FIVE

Appetite for Murder

"But here is your snag, Wimsey. When and how was the poison administered? . . . Urquhart's only opportunity was at the dinner he shared with Boyes, and if anything in this case is certain, it is that the poison was not administered at that dinner. Everything which Boyes ate or drank was equally eaten and drunk by Urquhart and the servants . . ."

"I know," said Wimsey, "but that is what is so suspicious."

DOROTHY L. SAYERS, *Strong Poison*

Say what you will, poison's the best way. If only because it serves as a prelude to the plate. When there's a poisoning, there will be recipes for mushroom soup. Discussions of curry. What to do with the leftovers. Platters piled with oysters. If it weren't for poison, we'd rarely hear a fork fall. Or, at least, never get quite the same chance to savor the series of spoon-licking ceremonials that lead up to it. Contemplate the ingredients. Hear how they were put together. Find food the object of interest for every gripping page. The perfect complements: mystery and menus. Anxiety titillator, anxiety cure.

Food is in its element in a mystery. Eliciting revelations. Bucking up the bereaved. Lending an air of reality to the proceedings. But never does it come into its own as it does in a poisoning. Many are the menus mapped out for murder delicious enough to risk death for.

Hidden within each mystery reader is a gourmet; guiding each stroke of the writer's pen is a *chef* of *chef d'oeuvres.* If mysteries contain menus and recipes for murder, happily they contain menus and recipes for meals as well. Between shudders of fear and apprehension at a past or coming crime are delightful islands where the principal consideration is the next dish, and the shudders are solely pleasurable. The aroma of herbs or fresh bread rises in the air, ginger cake lurks in the larder, a pan sizzles anticipating Yorkshire pudding, a bottle of burgundy makes a sound Margery Allingham describes in *Pearls Before Swine,* as a "ghost of a pop; . . . a beautiful sound, regretful, grateful, kind." The only thing for it is to pull up a spoon and sit down.

However, after the fourth omelet, gladly received, and the fifth plate of sole; after being told quails are awkward when an unexpected guest turns up for dinner, and two cup custards are impossible when a third person appears; after savoring the third caramel-beaded apple tart, and sharing Miss Marple's chagrin, during a period of invalidery, at the approach of a companion "with another egg dish"; after thinking "I must try that some time" when a recipe for cocoa with rum is given in Agatha Christie's *The Mysterious Affair at Styles* or drinking oneself blind on White Ladies after that deceptive charmer turns killer in Carter Dickson's hands; and admiring the seventh platter of scones dripping butter and honey, one stops to wonder "why." Why, and wherefore, all the food?

The answer can be delightful. In Miss Christie's "The Adventure of the Christmas Pudding," food becomes a hiding place. The Christmas pudding has all the required ingredients: a silver bachelor's button, a ruby red stone, a pig, an old maid's thimble, a gold ten shilling piece, and another ring. A fabulous jewel is masquerading as the ruby red stone. In Miss Christie's "Four-and-Twenty Blackbirds," food is a trap. The murderer, impersonating his uncle, is detected because he orders a thick tomato soup, beefsteak and kidney pudding and blackberry tart at his uncle's club, when "he never could bear suet pudding or blackberries and I've never known him take thick soup." Also, the victim's teeth are not stained by the blackberries he is supposed to have eaten!

In cases of suspected or proven poisoning, the reason is apparent: to discover how the poison was administered. But during a crime of violence or other crimes where food has no direct use? Why is the author whetting our appetites, indulging our taste for security with a hot and succulent dish, pampering us with the rewarding presence of a little something?

Writing about food, like reading about food, is an agreeable pastime, but mystery books are mystery books, and happy as their authors may be to indulge us, mysteries are not meant to be too literally a mental meal. The descriptions of food, the concentration on cuisine serve other purposes.

For a start, food indicates setting. When the scene is a country weekend at the Great House, or the aristocratic detective's Mayfair flat, the type of food served and the attention paid it are a means, as the presence of valet or gun room, Chippendale chairs or walls of chinoiserie, of enhancing the setting, of telling us we are in the atmosphere of affluence, for the affluent have at their disposal the implements of decadence. Enough time, servants, and money to make food, not a means of sustenance and survival, but an art form, a way of titillating, and giving hedonistic pleasure. An *entrecôte béarnaise* and a *savarin au rhum* announce the approach of an aristocrat, as clearly as a plate of sausage and mash say the police are here. In such manner, Dorothy Sayers rounds out her picture of upper-class life with plates and spoons. Agatha Christie amplifies her portrait of Poirot, as a man from the notoriously food-conscious French culture.

Food serves still another purpose. Although Josephine Tey's Inspector Grant is no gourmet, every bite and chew of a bap in *The Singing Sands* is presented with gusto. This is not, says the bap, a story being told; this is real life. In mysteries, food is, in fact, one of the few means of creating an impression of life. Emotions are avoided; even physical realities are kept at a minimum. People don't breathe, except their last; they have hysterics, but they rarely cry; only the most suspicious characters sweat; bathrooms are merely places where baths are drawn and pills are switched. In short, food serves an important function in giving a sense of reality.

But attention to food goes beyond the merely serviceable. The descriptions are given, not quickly, as if to perform an office and move on; they are not perfunctory; they are nothing less than lascivious. The author is clearly enjoying herself. She is tasting, smelling, eating every morsel. She has put in her thumb, and pulled out a plum.

"It is also true, of course," says Dr. Karl Menninger, one of the least subject of any modern-day psychologist to imaginative flights, "that eating has an unconscious aggressive meaning which extends back to the primitive customs of devouring one's enemies." Whether it is necessary to go back to the cannibal's "a human being in every pot" for precedence, eating, devouring, has obviously aggressive origins. One need only conjure up the familiar vision of Henry the Eighth gnawing bones and tossing them over his shoulder at snarling dogs, then, to ask oneself if eating is *not* an aggressive act. Caesar had his wits about him when he said to keep a weather-eye on thin people. Thin people, if Caesar was a good psychologist, are more likely to have their aggressions directed at the outside world, while heavy people are their own arena, fighting their battles between teeth and stomach.

To deny the aggressiveness inherent in a mystery book whose subject, however muted, is murder, even though they are read by excessively moral people, would be ridiculous. Eating, like reading mysteries, is another acceptable way of releasing aggressions. Dorothy Sayers has pointed out in her introduction to *The Third Omnibus of Crime* that "bishops, schoolmasters, eminent statesmen and others with reputations to support, read detective stories, to improve their morals and keep themselves out of mischief." If, amusing as it is, it is inaccurate to say that the highly reputable read mysteries to *improve* their morals, it is no less than probable that they read mysteries to support the morals they already have, thereby keeping themselves out of mischief. Mysteries support the righteous in their righteousness. With a mystery, a man of too-sensitive conscience can safely employ his aggressive instincts, and keep himself in what he considers the proper moral balance. The hare we hunt is a murderer, but still, it is we who hunt; vigorously, because our cause is just. As he reads, the minister may let his fangs grow, vicariously enjoying the savage delight of murder, knowing that virtue will triumph and evil be punished in time for the Sunday sermon, thus proving the cost of controlling his aggressions is worth it.

The prevalence of the platter in the mystery, like the mystery itself, is an embellishment, a cheerful flourish, a civilized façade on one of man's most basic instincts: aggression.

"Here is a book of . . . stories designed to make you feel that it is good to be alive and that, while alive, it is better on the whole to be good," says Miss Sayers of the stories in *The Third Omnibus of Crime*, but it could apply equally well to all mysteries. It is good to be alive, and probably better to be good, but it is best of all to be rewarded with a heaping platter before you.

TWENTY-SIX

The Deadly Dull Palate

"Didn't he notice the taste?"
"He must have done. The famous palate can't have
been as bad as that, but he took it at a gulp, you see."
MARGERY ALLINGHAM, *Pearls Before Swine*

If you have a taste for murder, prefer a victim who has none.
Fortunately, something happens to victims. Out of a subcon-
scious wish to be helpful, apparently they lose the senses they
had, and undergo a kind of blight of the taste buds. Even the
gourmet, when being primed for murder, seems incapable of
discernment. The most stirring outcry he can muster, as he slides
out of sight beneath the table (because poison has been positive-
ly ladled into his soup), is, "that tastes a bit queer." Surely no
gourmet worth his arsenic salts could be wiped out with such
ease. Alarm bells should ring all along his palate, forks fly and,
with them, strong words. But even when the victim's taste buds
are ordinarily acute, he virtually swallows things whole, or at
one gulp on this occasion. Not properly brought up. Score one

for mothers who stop children from putting things in their mouths whole, and make them chew each bite thirty-two times. It never does to be piggy when poison's on the menu. For the careful consumer, if one exists, the cautious poisoner chooses a dish with a riveting flavor like curry, a drink virile as coffee. Curry and coffee subdue the liveliest poisons.

When a poisoner's loose, you should definitely look a gift horse in the mouth, particularly if it's meant to be put in yours. Mistrust postmen bearing boxes of chocolates. Ten to one, they've had tiny holes drilled in the bottom of them, and every third one is poison-filled. This way, the would-be murderer can accept one, if offered, and still survive because the box is laid out according to his own checkerboard. If he has a favorite flavor, he can arrange that none of these is poisoned. Moreover, if he's thorough, and all murderers are, the poisoner knows his victim's favorite, too, to insure that she heads like a homing pigeon for the swirled O's signifying orange, or those sentimentally topped with candied violets.

There are three principal types of poisoner. The don't-care-who-knows-it murderer who doctors the victim's food (just a few more crunchy foxglove leaves in that salad. Ah, perfect!) or drink, who is, nevertheless, cautious enough to be basking on the Riviera by the time the victim hits the bottom of the decanter of port where a little something has dissolved. The second, or crafty murderer, who attempts to make death appear to be from natural causes, the result of an accidental overdose of a required medicine, or a suicide. The really devious murderer who poisons himself for appearance's sake, either to look like an intended victim himself, by nibbling on a souvenir piece of heavily frosted and poisoned wedding cake, or to inure himself to the poison he will consume with the victim.

A hardened criminal like the last-mentioned requires a sweet tooth and a Wimsey to catch him. In Dorothy Sayers's *Strong Poison*, the Wimsical method is to offer the suspected arsenicker a plate full of Turkish delight and say, as the suspect dusts off his lips after the last bite, "Oh, by the way, Old Horse, that was a new recipe. Did you fancy it? Arsenic instead of powdered sugar." Then, Wimsey suggests that to prove his innocence, the murderer had better be very quickly sick. An arsenicker's lot is not a happy one. One so often hazards this type of tasteless joke.

Demise by poison has innumerable advantages, apart from the opportunity to think about food. Not only can it be made to look natural, it is quieter, if less forthright, than shooting, and so easy a woman can do it. No muss, no fuss. Just open the bedroom door in the morning, and there is the victim, as it were, sleeping peacefully.

Poison is also less offensive than strangulation and bludgeoning, is more naturally mysterious, and requires infinitely more pains to trace. When one is shot in the head, there's an end of it. Nor can there be much question about a solid bash in the temple. Or a dip, when you're not in bathing trunks. If there is a question, it will take more than the examination of the doctor or detective to determine that, in point of fact, the victim was dead *before* he was shot or fell in the drink. Almost the entire book can be spent attempting to discover whether or not the victim was, in fact, poisoned. Always had a ticky tummy, don't y'know. Or tended to grow yellow at night. Or blow phosphorus haloes after soup. Or fall lifeless in his coffee spoon. Poor old type. Never mind about that. Pass the gravy.

TWENTY-SEVEN

Survival of the Fittest

"Well, look after yourself," said Craddock warningly. "There's a poisoner in this house, remember, and one of your patients upstairs probably isn't as ill as he pretends to be."

AGATHA CHRISTIE, *What Mrs. McGillicuddy Saw*

Murderers, in common with other people, do not always succeed. Which is a comfort. Sometimes an attempt by poisoning goes astray. No other attempt does. Wounding with knife, fork, or gun might imply bad aim, a possibility insulting to the sporting blood of England. And a would-be victim, in such cases, is a lot more likely to see who-done-it.

While the would-be victim holes up in bed to await his next turn, plaintively nibbling his toast and tea, and nursing a beginning persecution complex, the murderer-to-be festers down the hall plotting a return engagement. A shiftless nurse can accommodate the latter by stepping away from the bed for a moment's chat with the cook, thus affording him another opportunity to strike by switching pills or jimmying the hypodermic needle. If murder's to be done, nurses with a past—a case of unexplained death in another town—should be sought. Suspicion will fall on them instantly. An urgent telephone call can take away a conscientious nurse, providing time to diddle the pill bottles or replace an innocuous stomach potion with a permanent fix-it. Murderers are extremely competent in matters medical and, but for a wrong turn, might have benefited mankind enormously. If decoying the nurse seems risky, it may be easier to slip a little something on the invalid tray. A trace of arsenic in hot milk, for example, goes down well.

If the tray is left for a moment, a quick dart from a nearby room, *et voilà!* fixilated milk. Otherwise, there is always jostling on the stairs. "Oh, I do beg your pardon, Miss Wray. Did the milk get spilled? Oh, here are the pills, they seem to have rolled under the stair." With a modicum of charm on the murderer's part, the approach can be a request to help the nurse by carrying the tray to the patient; the kind of gentle charm that makes the nurse say all the way from the depth of her wobbly knees, "Of course, take the aging, sick, fabulously wealthy widow her tray for me." The same type of charm makes it possible, if you'd prefer not to chloroform an aging benefactress, to hold out her smelling salts with a winning smile, and a full load of cyanide in their stead. Smells good, and the effects are absolutely heady.

What with one thing and another, there are a large number of invalids in murder mysteries. Of these, there are four principal categories: those temporarily inactivated by a legitimate attempt on their lives; the murderer who is foxing; those who've made invaliding a lifelong work, and may not be half as feeble as they'd like us to believe; and the invalid-with-a-will, whom age alone has brought down.

Caused invalidery (frequent) is a temporary-to-permanent condition depending on the murderer's speed and tenacity, which beds down a normally healthy person with the after-effects of an attempt. A murderer may sicken a whole table of guests in order to fell one. Poisoning and snow are responsible for more isolated weekend guests than any other causes. The guardian in love with his ward in Agatha Christie's "The Herb of Death," gives his guests duck stuffed with sage and foxglove leaves (i.e., the heart medicine, digitalis) for dinner, which makes them all ill. He kills his ward, however, by the judicious application of an extra dose of plain digitalis to her cocktail.

The second category of invalid includes the near-victim who is actually the murderer, and has deliberately brought himself to the brink of death in order to convince any onlookers that he is himself a target. Any detective worth his salt will, of course, not be deceived. He observes the unholy smoothness of hair and skin, indicative of more than a slick operator, or the rude ruffling of the skin's pigment. He hurries off to the murderer-victim's barbershop or bathroom and gathers locks of hair with telltale traces of poison at the roots, which would be the envy of any acquisitive witch. Then, to clinch his case, he sidles up to the *soi-disant* victim's manicurist for nail parings.

In the third category of invalidery are those who, having discovered early a preference for lying about and being fussed over rather than working, choose to make invaliding a life's work. Such a man is Timothy Abernathy in Agatha Christie's *Funerals Are Fatal*. "His invalid status was emphasised by the rug across his knees and a positive pharmacopeia of little bottles and boxes on a table at his right hand.

"'I mustn't exert myself,' he said warningly. 'Doctor's forbidden it. Keeps telling me not to worry! Worry! If *he'd* had a murder in his family *he'd* do a bit of worrying.' . . . In his excitement Timothy had kicked aside his rug and had sat up in his chair. There were no signs of weakness or fragility about him. He looked . . . a perfectly healthy man, even if a slightly excitable one." In such cases, one is left to wonder if the invalid summoned enough strength, after twenty bedridden years, to run down two flights of stairs and up again, in time to brutally stab a vigorous youth, and yet be all tucked up in his covers and peacefully pale when the nurse came back with the lunch tray.

This kind of invalid, when not actually eating, is thinking about it or complaining about what he just turned up his nose at: a skin on the hot milk, a lumpy macaroni cheese, being given digestive biscuits instead of gingernuts or beef tea instead of beefsteak. Though incapacitated, he is not so incapacitated he can't bully the servants, convert his tweedy, serviceable wife into a nanny, and eat with ferocious appetite. He will have every meal plus elevenses.

The fourth category of invalid is the victim with a will—legal—or a safe in the wall behind her bed. She is a very old lady, propped up on pillows, who absolutely cries out to be stifled with one of them, for chloroform taken neat, or to have her soup flavored with phosphorus to wreck her liver. Her room is high-ceilinged and dim, with dusty artifacts of her life, and a velvet pull to summon, except *in extremis*, an almost equally aged maid from the bowels of the Great House. In such cases, paper and pencil are placed with a nice foresight by the bed, so that a cryptic message can be written on it and destroyed, leaving just enough imprinted on the next sheet of paper to tantalize the detective.

Doctors loom large in poisoning. Despite their stalwart manner, and the same reliable solidity one encounters in a police inspector, doctors make the best poisoners, and very respectable murderers as well. A doctor knows his dosages, and usually has them handy in his little black bag, so there's no need of telltale trips to the chemist's that are always so memorable. As he is sure to be called in on the case, he can get rid of any clumsy traces of his activities, or can kill while curing. The doctor-poisoner in Agatha Christie's *What Mrs. McGillicuddy Saw* poisons six in order to prescribe something fatal for one. Extreme, perhaps, but worth a try. A doctor also has a strong, steady, cool hand with which to give a hypodermic needle, and has that confidence-inspiring bedside manner that allows him to draw near the patient and put a pillow over her face.

Then, too, the doctor is so trustworthy. He knows more secrets than anyone in the village. More secrets by far than the vicar, who misses most of the last confessions of his parishioners because he has gone to the wrong house. Also, the vicar's unworldliness makes him unable to comprehend the problems of everyday living, and his parishioners are too shy and uncomfortable to explain. The doctor, on the other hand, sees all and hears more. He has attended the characters all their lives because he began to practice medicine when he was six, and knows all the local skeletons by their first names. If, as in Agatha Christie's *The Murder of Roger Ackroyd*, a rather sympathetic woman has seen fit to poison her husband fatally (he drank), the doctor is johnny-on-the-spot as recognizing it, and taking ungentlemanly advantage of his knowledge to the tune of a few hundred quid per annum.

Even if the doctor is a rather old and deaf country doctor, after sufficient ruminating—a long, labored week should do it—he will begin to realize he heard something that doesn't quite add up and, in fact, there was something unusual about the deep blue of the patient's face, the rope around his throat, and the large container of rat poison in the corner of the room. With his newfound insight, the doctor may (1) hurry to the police (2) ruminate some more, and ask the murderer his opinion (3) forget about it. In the last case, someone else may begin to reflect, and initiate an investigation. Even a murderer can want his victims unearthed on occasion to prove he couldn't possibly have done it, or any other in the long series of murders that came after. Murderers never take a straight path when they can take a crooked. They prefer the circuitous approach; it's endemic. And given a pathway or a flowerbed, a murderer will naturally walk through the flowerbed. Force of habit. The police could save themselves a lot of trouble if they ran simple road tests, rather like the balloon alcohol tests for drivers, to see how suspects take their paths.

When you add to that doctors whose noses have been impaired by flu so that they can't smell cyanide, confidence undergoes a strain.

Therefore, in case of illness, do not call a doctor. If he is not senile or otherwise incapacitated, he is probably the murderer. All the little old ladies in town, the modern descendants of witches, can offer better cures from their vast lore. Miss Marple, for example, uses leeches, black draught, and camphorated oil for coughs and, for all else, her grandmother's tansy tea receipt, which is "worth any amount of your drugs." Invalid food will do the rest.

† THE INVALID TRAY

Most important, of course, is that the invalid tray be almost hopelessly bland. But within that limitation, it can and will tickle the tremulous appetite of someone who might reasonably be expected to cast a suspicious eye on his food. It should be presented in a palatable and tempting way. A sprightly cover on the tray. A small clutch of flowers—daisies or zinnias, perhaps; nothing funereal. Don't sing "Whistle While It Works." It might be misconstrued, and should a card arrive for the victim reading "Having a wonderful crime, wish you were here," however well-meant, destroy it. A chipper smile on the nurse's face, accompanied by soothing noises, though the use of "we" as in "don't *we* want our nice bowl of gruel?" seems to offend more patients than it pleases. Finally, all dishes of invalid food, to be authentic, must be prefaced by "nice," as in "nice cup custard," "nice beef tea," "nice macaroni cheese." No other kind can cure.

INVALID TRAY FOR ONE
> *Beef tea*
> *Avgolemono*
> *Rum Junket*
> *Madeira Jelly*
> *Milk Toast*
> *A Nice Custard*
> *Flummery*
> *Barley water*

† BEEF TEA

Admittedly most people will dissolve Bovril or a bouillon cube in boiling water to get beef tea, but real beef tea is quite another matter.

1 lb freshly ground chuck	1 stalk celery, sliced
1 very small onion, sliced	½ tsp salt
½ small carrot, sliced	2½ cups water

Put all the ingredients in a casserole with a tight cover. Mix well. Cook in a 275° F oven for 3 to 4 hours. Strain off the broth into a bowl and when it is cool put it in the refrigerator. Remove all the fat that coagulates at the top. Season to taste before serving.

† AVGOLEMONO

1½ cups clear chicken broth	1 egg yolk
2 tbsp cooked rice	1 tbsp lemon juice

Heat the broth with the rice. Blend the egg yolk with the lemon juice, and whisk in ½ cup of the chicken broth. Whisk this mixture in with the rest of the broth, heating it thoroughly but not letting it boil. Serve immediately.

† RUM JUNKET

This hardly needs a recipe, but the result is apt to perk up the invalid.

1¾ cups thin cream or rich milk   ¼ cup light rum
                                    1 package junket mix

Warm the cream and rum just to lukewarm. Whisk in a package of junket mix and pour into custard cups. Let stand until cool. Chill.

† MADEIRA JELLY
(*2 to 3 servings*)

1 package gelatine   ⅛ tsp salt
¼ cup cold water   2 tbsp orange juice
¾ cup boiling water   1 tbsp lemon juice
½ cup sugar   ½ cup madeira

Soak the gelatine in cold water. Add the boiling water, sugar, and salt and stir until the gelatine is dissolved. Add the fruit juice and wine. Stir, and pour into individual bowls. Cool, and then chill in the refrigerator.

† MILK TOAST

Cut a thick slice of bread and toast it on both sides. Spread with butter. Place in a soup plate, and cover with 1 cup of scalded milk or light cream. Season with salt and, if allowed, with pepper.

† A NICE CUSTARD

2 eggs	2 cups scalded milk
1 egg yolk	1 tsp vanilla extract
½ cup sugar	nutmeg
⅛ tsp salt	

Preheat the oven to 350° F. Beat the eggs, sugar, and salt until just blended. Add the scalded milk gradually, beating constantly. Add the vanilla and pour into 4 lightly buttered custard cups. Sprinkle with nutmeg and place in a pan of hot water deep enough to come almost to the level of the tops of the cups. Bake 40 minutes or until a knife inserted in the custard comes out clean. Remove the cups from the water to cool. Chill before serving.

† FLUMMERY

1 package (1 tbsp) gelatine	¼ cup sugar
1¼ cups water	⅛ tsp salt
½ lemon	1 egg
4 tbsp sherry	

Soften the gelatine in ¼ cup of the water, then stir into the rest of the water in the top of a small double boiler. Grate the lemon rind and add to the gelatine and water. Cook over simmering water for 10 minutes, stirring until all the gelatine has dissolved. Add the juice of the ½ lemon, the sherry, sugar, and salt, and stir until the sugar has dissolved. Beat the egg lightly and add to it 2 tbsp of the hot mixture, stirring constantly. Add this egg mixture to the hot gelatine gradually, stirring it over the simmering water until it begins to thicken. Pour into two bowls and, when cool, chill it in the refrigerator. Eat the same day because this dessert toughens if allowed to stand too long.

† *BARLEY WATER*

¼ cup pearl barley rind of ½ lemon
1 tbsp sugar   1¼ cups boiling water

Put the barley in a small pan. Cover with cold water. Bring to a boil and boil 3 minutes. Drain and place the barley in a glass jar. Add the sugar and lemon rind and pour in the boiling water. Let stand until cool.

TWENTY-EIGHT

The Post-Funeral Lunch: Where There's a Will, There's a Way

Extraordinary how hungry a funeral made you feel. The soup at Enderby had been delicious—and so was the cold soufflé.

AGATHA CHRISTIE, *Funerals Are Fatal*

Funerals are family affairs; they draw together brothers, sisters, nieces, nephews, and their husbands and wives, who haven't seen each other in years. Funerals are worth having only if the Old Party was old enough to have accumulated a large family and a larger amount of money. Funerals are even snugger and more inbred than country weekends, thus providing the ideal, closed society of the mystery. They can also be jollier than a country weekend because death has already been and gone (and everyone feels the better for it), which cuts down on the probability of screams, hastily flung-on dressing gowns, and thudding feet in the night, at least for a while. And once the proprieties of long faces and black crepe are dispensed with, the atmosphere can become quite rollicking.

While the family is gathered at the interment, Old Dodders, the butler, lost in reveries of the past, totters about rooms hung with faded brocades and velvets, pulling up the blinds that closed the mourning windows, and thinking how seedy the younger generation looks. Though he and other members of the staff attended the funeral, they have come back before the family to prepare the house for its return, to light the fires, draw the blinds, and prepare lunch.

Below stairs in the kitchen, much to the butler's dismay, the staff will be enjoying reminiscences of a rather different character from his own sentimental ones. The rest of the staff is voluptuously reliving the events of the day, the full-hearted savoring of a really good funeral. The lavish display of flowers. The large number of fine cars. The beauty of the weather. The array of important people. And, of course, the eulogies, dripping with lovely feelings that made you proud to have been in service at Old Skinflint's, delivered in suitably unctuous tones by the canon.

The cook, stirring a large saucepan of delicious cock-a-leeky soup, may even be so moved as to require a pause to brush away a pleasurable tear, and have another cup of sweet, inky tea. The servants are certain to have gotten far more pleasure from the occasion than the family. For one thing, as we know, the lower classes give way to their feelings, and enjoy it; and for sheer spectacle, there's been nothing to beat funerals since old bread-and-circus days. For another, the servants may have a soft spot for the Old Codger (they don't make 'em like that any more), which the heirs most assuredly do not. The family is more likely to be annoyed that he's hung on this long. One of them, in particular. As servants always get a little legacy (even the worst Old Codgers don't cut off their servants), there is also an atmosphere of agreeable anticipation mixed with the succulent odors of cooking.

While the soup simmers, and the maids snuffle happily, a crunch of wheels on the driveway announces the family's return. Their welcome is prepared. The fire, burning cheerily in the drawing-room grate, takes the chill off the room and the occasion. Any lingering traces are taken away by the butler's entrance with glasses and sherry on a silver tray.

If the family returns subdued, it is from more than a feeling for the proprieties. Their minds are elsewhere: buying yachts, betting on horses, renting villas on the Riviera, opening up art galleries, putting their sons through public school—whatever their heretofore-thwarted bent soon to be loosed by a legacy. The drawing room will be almost hazy with dreams brinking on realization, colliding like balloons battling for air space. No one present must be overfond of the deceased; it would ruin the fun and make the reader uncomfortable.

After the funeral is the moment for the lightest lunch. Nothing heavy nor difficult. Someone might be making an effort to be sad. More will be edgy because the reading of the will follows the sweet. Also, Cook will have been at the services. There should be no little French sauces to draw attention to themselves, and the pleasure of eating them. This could make one aware that he is not eating simply out of necessity, but enjoying it, and about to ask for more.

A soufflé is never more perfect, an *assiette anglaise*—the plate of handsomely arranged cold meats—never more appreciated. A chicken in half mourning might be considered crowing on the part of those who have so obviously only profited by the occasion. Such a dish, however, is the sort of thing one might expect from a murderer who, with traditional conceit, can't resist his little joke.

By the sweet course, the tide will definitely have turned, and the family given way to undisguised enjoyment of their lunch, the cool Chablis, and a few light-hearted recollections. While Old Dodders dreams, moist-eyed, of Miss Lucy when she was a winsome girl, the family is chuckling, with the corpulent fifty-year-old she has become, over the time they tried to lower her into the well, or when they walled her up in the pantry. The stimulus of the coming reading of the will brings an even rosier flush to the cheeks.

After lunch, the family moves into the library, where a wealth of old bindings lends its aura of tradition and solemnity, and the butler, with his usual sense of the niceties, brings the coffee. A gathering for the reading of the will early in the book is always a good opportunity to go into the characters of those assembled through the thoughts of the lawyer down from London, who has known the family since Skinflint was a boy (lawyers are remarkably long-lived). His thoughts delineate them like pawns on a chessboard.

Lawyers are so gray you hardly even notice they're there except for the occasional flashes of light on their pince-nez. You're only *sure* they've been there by a raft of codicils left in their wake. Lawyers are everything you think they are: fidgety, precise, and dry. They are as close-mouthed as other confessors —the doctor and the vicar—and also, as they're located in town, hidden behind clerks in their offices, it's hard to get anything out of them. But to compensate, they have delightful old sets of rooms in Staple Inn, where they serve excellent saddles of mutton, and port left them by a strange old client who kept it past its prime because he believed nothing ever lives up to its expectation. House party guests suffer more from being unable to get to town to see their solicitors than from being locked up in the same house with a murderer.

The reading of the will invariably unseats someone's expectations. The old devil, Skinflint, having noticed a certain arsenical brown about his porridge of late, and the subsequent misbehavior of his stomach, will unaccountably have lingered long enough to get himself killed, but also cannily shuffled the order of his will just enough to make it necessary for the murderer to do a little more spadework before resting on his laurels. Often, the murderer planned such a little divertissement anyway, to point suspicion at someone else. It is a rare and lucky victim who is killed on his own merits and not as a means to another end, or to cover up another crime.

Wills make it possible for the old servants to retire, possibly to one of the outbuildings. The splendid Victorian pile itself is always left, rather than to the heir who adores it, to someone who doesn't care tuppence for it and will sell it forthwith. The monies bequeathed are put in trust with an income for life for the ladies to revert to the estate on their deaths; and shared out equally among the men. Or everything is given to someone outside the family, who has been kind to Skinflint—or to a medium who helped put him in touch with his young daughter, Goldilocks, long since Passed Over, which will really make them peevish. That person had better look to his or her porridge. All the heirs now itch to get their hands on the Old Codger. Unfortunately, you cannot be murdered twice for the same crime.

THE POST-FUNERAL LUNCH
   (for six to eight persons)

These light luncheon dishes make a festive occasion of a simple gathering of friends who have nothing heavier on their minds than the joy of living.

Antipasto
Cock-a-Leeky
Iced Cucumber-Tarragon Soup
Mushroom-Madeira Soup
Chicken Liver and Mushroom Omelet

Fish and Cheese Soufflé
Seafood Coquilles
Prawn Mousse
Chicken in Tarragon Jelly
Chicken Breasts in Half Mourning
Dublin Steak
Spinach Timbales
Zucchini Casserole
Cabbage Salad with Cooked Dressing
Artichoke Hearts Vinaigrette
Jam Roll Pudding
Brandy Snap Rolls
Lemon Pancakes with Summer Sauce

† ANTIPASTO

Line individual salad plates with leaf lettuce and on it put four or more of the following items, or others that this list may suggest to you. Have oil and vinegar cruets and salt and pepper mills on the table, and serve with plenty of French or Italian bread.

sliced salami	Italian or Greek olives
prosciutto, or thinly sliced cooked ham	raw mushrooms, marinated in a vinaigrette sauce
very young, very fresh raw asparagus	sliced raw green peppers
scallions	Italian hot Tuscan peppers
sliced raw fennel	Italian canned fried peppers
sliced cooked beets	anchovies
marinated artichoke hearts	chunk tuna fish
sliced tomatoes	shrimps, or canned mussels or clams

† COCK-A-LEEKY

Start this a day before serving.

1 bunch (4 to 6) leeks	2 quarts canned bouillon
1 3-lb chicken	salt and pepper

Remove the roots and the green part of the leeks, and wash thoroughly. Cut them into pieces about 1¼ inches long, and slice into thin sticks. Wash the chicken inside and out, and remove any excess fat. Bind the wings and legs to the body with kitchen twine. Place the chicken in a kettle with the bouillon and add a handful of the leek sticks. Bring the soup to a boil over a moderately high heat, skimming off any scum that rises to the top. Simmer 45 minutes. Add the rest of the leeks and simmer 1½ hours longer. Remove the chicken from the soup, let both cool and refrigerate overnight uncovered.

The next day remove all fat that has coagulated on the top of the soup. Remove the meat from the bones of the chicken and cut into thin strips like the leek sticks. Add them to the soup and reheat. Season with salt and pepper.

† ICED CUCUMBER-TARRAGON SOUP

2 tsp fresh tarragon, chopped	3 tbsp flour
4 cups chicken bouillon	green coloring
½ tsp dried tarragon	1 cup heavy cream
4 cucumbers	salt and white pepper
1 medium onion chopped fine	chopped fresh tarragon or
3 tbsp butter	parsley

Simmer the tarragon in the chicken bouillon for 15 minutes. Meanwhile peel, seed, and dice the cucumbers. Put them with the onion and butter into a covered pan and cook over moderate heat until soft, about 10 minutes. Add the flour and stir for 2 to 3 minutes. Strain the chicken broth into the cucumbers and simmer for 10 minutes. Cool. Add a few drops of green vegetable coloring. Put in a blender, and blend until smooth. Add the cream and season highly with salt and pepper. Chill thoroughly and serve with a garnish of chopped fresh tarragon or parsley.

† *MUSHROOM-MADEIRA SOUP*

½ lb mushrooms	2 cups chicken bouillon
6 tbsp butter	salt and pepper
2 tbsp chopped onion	½ pint heavy cream
4 tbsp flour	½ tsp lemon juice
2 cups milk	2 tbsp madeira

Wash, trim, and chop the mushrooms finely. Melt the butter and cook the onion in it over moderate heat until soft. Add the mushrooms and cook 3 minutes. Sprinkle with the flour and stir until the flour has disappeared. Add the milk and bouillon gradually, stir until smooth and simmer 10 minutes. Season with salt and pepper. Just before serving, add the cream, lemon juice, and madeira and reheat without boiling.

† *CHICKEN LIVER AND MUSHROOM OMELET*

All experts agree that it is better to make three 4-egg omelets than one 12-egg omelet. Provide yourself with an 8 to 9 inch pan with sloping sides which is used exclusively for omelets. One of these omelets will serve 2 to 3 people. Prepare the filling and make the omelets on demand.

FILLING	OMELETS
6 tbsp butter	12 eggs
6 chicken livers, cut in 4 pieces	¼ cup water
2 tbsp chopped onion	1 tsp salt
¼ lb mushrooms, trimmed and sliced	freshly ground
1 tbsp flour	black pepper
½ cup chicken bouillon	butter
2 tbsp sherry	3 tbsp chopped
1 tsp lemon juice	parsley
½ cup heavy cream	
salt and pepper	

FILLING: Heat 4 tbsp butter in a skillet and brown the chicken livers over high heat for 1½ minutes, stirring so that the livers are browned on the outside but still rather pink inside. Remove from the butter with a slotted spoon and put in the top of a double boiler. Reduce the heat, add 2 tbsp of butter and cook the onions and mushrooms together until the onions are soft. Sprinkle with the flour and stir until the flour disappears. Add the bouillon, sherry, and lemon juice and stir until blended. Add the cream and taste for seasoning. Add the mixture to the livers and keep warm.

OMELETS: Beat the eggs and water until blended. Add the salt and pepper. Heat the omelet pan and add 1 tbsp butter, tilting the pan as the butter melts so that it is well coated. Pour in ⅓ of the egg mixture. Let is cook a moment, and then prick it in several places to let the uncooked egg seep through. While still moist on the top put ⅓ of the filling on one half of the omelet. Fold over the other half with a spatula and roll the omelet onto a warm platter. Keep warm. Repeat the process twice. Serve garnished with parsley.

† FISH AND CHEESE SOUFFLÉ

8 tbsp butter or margarine	¼ lb medium sharp Cheddar
12 tbsp flour	cheese, grated
2½ cups milk	1 tbsp grated onion
1½ cups cooked, flaked white	1½ tsp salt
fish (cod, haddock, halibut)	½ tsp white pepper
	8 eggs

Heat the butter in a heavy saucepan and stir in the flour. Cook without browning for 2 or 3 minutes. Add half the milk and stir until smooth. Add the rest and continue stirring until thick. Remove from the heat and add the fish and cheese, onion, and seasoning. Mix thoroughly.

Separate the egg yolks from the whites. Beat the yolks for 2 minutes and add to the mixture. Preheat the oven to 350° F. Beat the egg whites until fairly stiff. Stir in a quarter of the whites very thoroughly and fold in the rest gently. Place the mixture in a large buttered, straight-sided soufflé dish or casserole. Place the dish in a pan of hot water and bake 1¼ hours.

The first part of the preparation can be made in advance. Just before baking add the egg whites.

† SEAFOOD COQUILLES

8 tbsp butter or margarine	6 tbsp flour
2 cups (12 oz) frozen	1 cup milk
langostinos or cooked cleaned shrimp	1 cup chicken
1 small onion, minced	bouillon
¼ lb mushrooms	2 tbsp dry vermouth
½ pint scallops	1 tsp lemon juice
1 cup dry white wine	salt and pepper
	soft bread crumbs
	chopped parsley

Heat 3 tbsp butter in a skillet and gently sauté the thawed langostinos or shrimp for 5 minutes, stirring occasionally. Transfer the shellfish to a bowl. Add 1 tbsp butter to the skillet and sauté gently for 3 minutes the minced onion and the mushrooms which have been trimmed, washed, and sliced. Do not brown. Transfer them to the bowl with the shellfish. Simmer the scallops in the white wine for 3 to 4 minutes. Remove from the pan with a slotted spoon. Reserve the liquid. Cut the scallops into pieces and add them to the other shellfish.

Add 2 more tbsp butter to the skillet, and when melted add the flour. Stir well for 1 to 2 minutes to cook the flour. Do not brown. Add the liquid from the scallops, the milk, chicken bouillon, vermouth, and lemon juice, and stir until smooth. Season with salt and pepper. Strain the mixture into the bowl containing the shellfish and stir gently.

Place the mixture in scallop shells or individual ramekins. Cover with soft bread crumbs and dot with butter. Bake 15 to 20 minutes at 375° F. Before serving, garnish with a piece of langostino or shrimp reserved for the purpose and sprinkle with chopped parsley.

† PRAWN MOUSSE

MOUSSE	SAUCE
2 cups cleaned cooked prawns or shrimp	3 egg yolks
2 tsp lemon juice	2 tsp flour
1 tbsp minced shallots	3 tbsp cream
¾ tsp salt	1½ tbsp lemon juice
¼ tsp white pepper	6 tbsp butter
½ cup all-purpose cream	½ cup cooked prawn
3 egg whites, beaten stiff	or shrimp
	¼ cup slivered almonds
	salt and pepper
	1 tbsp chopped parsley

Cut the shrimp in pieces and spin in an electric blender with the lemon juice, shallots, salt, pepper, and cream. The resulting paste should be soft and fluffy.

Preheat the oven to 350° F.

Fold in the beaten egg whites and place the mixture in a buttered 1½ quart soufflé dish. Place the dish in a pan containing 3 inches of hot water. Bake 25 minutes.

SAUCE: Beat the egg yolks, flour, cream, and lemon juice until blended. Cook over a moderate heat beating constantly with a whisk until thick. Remove from the heat and beat in the butter 2 tbsp at a time, beating continuously. Add the shrimp, almonds, salt, and pepper according to taste. Spread some of the sauce gently over the soufflé and serve the rest in a separate bowl. Sprinkle the surface with chopped parsley.

† CHICKEN IN TARRAGON JELLY

2 broilers, quartered	1 onion, sliced
2 tsp fresh tarragon	1 stalk celery, sliced
or ½ tsp dried tarragon	1 tsp salt
1 cup dry white wine	⅛ tsp white pepper
½ cup water	chicken bouillon
	1 tbsp gelatine
	Kitchen Bouquet

Preheat the oven to 400° F. Place the chicken pieces in a casserole with the tarragon, wine, water, onion, celery, salt, and pepper. Cover tightly and bake for 45 to 50 minutes. The liquid coming from the chicken when pricked should be clear without a trace of pink. Take the chicken out of the casserole and strain the broth into a small bowl. Cool and chill both.

Later remove the fat from the bowl of liquid very carefully. Put the liquid in a measuring cup and add enough chicken bouillon to measure 2 cups. Heat. Soften the gelatine in ¼ cup of cold water and stir it into the liquid. Add a little Kitchen Bouquet to color it golden brown. Heat until the gelatine is thoroughly dissolved. Set aside to cool.

Remove the skin from the chicken and lay the pieces out on a platter. Place the pan containing the liquid in a bowl of ice and stir until it is slightly syrupy in consistency. Spoon the liquid over the chicken, covering each piece twice. Chill in the refrigerator. Before serving stir the jelly around the chicken with a fork to break it in little pieces. Garnish with fresh tarragon or, lacking that, with watercress or parsley.

† CHICKEN BREASTS IN HALF MOURNING

2 large truffles	2 tbsp butter
sherry	2 egg yolks
6 boned chicken breasts	1 tsp lemon juice
4 cups chicken broth	1 cup heavy cream
¼ lb large mushrooms	salt and white pepper

Cut each truffle in six slices and soak for 30 minutes in sherry. Lift the skin of each chicken breast and slip 2 truffle slices under it. Place the breasts in a shallow pan and just cover them with the broth. Cover and poach over moderate heat for 40 minutes.

Trim, wash, and slice the mushrooms. Cook them in butter until tender, stirring occasionally. Do not let them brown.

Remove the cooked chicken from the pan, cut away the skin but leave the truffles in place. Place on a serving platter and keep warm. Quickly boil down the chicken broth to a quantity of about 2 cups. Remove from the heat. Combine the egg yolks, lemon juice, and cream, add ½ cup of the hot broth, adding it gradually while stirring constantly. When well blended add the mixture to the rest of the stock. Reheat but do not boil. Taste for seasoning.

Place the mushrooms around the truffles and cover with a thin layer of sauce. Make sure the truffles and contrasting white mushrooms are in evidence, since they are the reason for the name. Serve the rest of the sauce in a gravy bowl.

† DUBLIN STEAK

3 tbsp vegetable oil	½ cup canned bouillon
4 lbs chuck or top round beef	2 cups stout
8 medium onions, chopped	2 tsp salt
2 tbsp flour	¼ tsp freshly ground pepper
2 tbsp brown sugar	1 bay leaf
	8 potatoes

Heat the oil in a Dutch oven or heavy saucepan. Add the meat cut in 2 inch cubes and cook until well browned. Remove the meat and set aside. Add the chopped onions and cook until slightly browned. Stir in the flour and sugar and cook until well browned. Stir in the bouillon and the stout. Bring to a boil. Return the meat to the pot, add salt and pepper and bay leaf. Cover tightly and simmer for 3 hours, or until the meat is tender. Peel and parboil the potatoes and add during the last half hour of cooking.

† SPINACH TIMBALES

2 boxes frozen, chopped spinach	1 tsp salt
½ cup boiling water	4 tbsp butter
1 tsp grated onion	4 eggs
6 tbsp soft bread crumbs	2 tbsp melted butter
¼ tsp nutmeg	4 tbsp grated Parmesan cheese
¼ tsp pepper	

Cook the spinach until just tender in ½ cup of boiling water and drain. There should be two full cups of spinach to make this dish. Combine the spinach with all the other ingredients, except for the last three, in a blender and spin to a purée. Preheat the oven to 350° F. Beat the eggs until light and stir them into the spinach. Pour into individual, buttered soufflé dishes or custard cups. Place them in a pan of hot water and bake until firm, approximately 30 minutes.

Unmold the timbales on a heated platter, sprinkle with the melted butter and Parmesan cheese.

† ZUCCHINI CASSEROLE

2 large or medium zucchini, cubed
1 large onion, diced or grated
4 tbsp butter
salt and pepper

1 pint sour cream
soft bread crumbs
2 tbsp melted butter
garlic salt (optional)

Cook the zucchini and onion in butter for 10 minutes, stirring frequently. Cool completely. Season with salt and pepper and stir in the sour cream. Place in a casserole. Sprinkle with bread crumbs, melted butter and, if you like, garlic salt. Bake 45 minutes at 300° F.

† CABBAGE SALAD WITH COOKED DRESSING

4 cups shredded cabbage
  SAUCE:
2 eggs, slightly beaten
1 tbsp sharp prepared mustard
2 tbsp flour

⅓ cup cider vinegar
1 tsp salt
1 tsp sugar
¾ cup cream
½ tsp celery seed

Soak the cabbage in ice water for at least an hour. Drain thoroughly. Combine all the ingredients for the sauce except celery seed in the top of a double boiler and stir over boiling water until it thickens. Pour into a nonmetal bowl and cool. Combine the cabbage and dressing and add the celery seed. Serve in a salad bowl.

† *ARTICHOKE HEARTS VINAIGRETTE*

Unless you live in artichoke country, use the frozen hearts.

3 boxes frozen artichoke hearts	**DRESSING**
1 pint cherry tomatoes	2 tbsp red wine vinegar
½ pint Greek black olives	6 tbsp olive oil
2 tbsp chopped green onions	½ tsp salt
½ knob fennel, chopped	black pepper

Boil the artichoke hearts until just tender. Undercook rather than overcook them. Rinse in cold water and drain well. Combine them with the tomatoes in a nonmetal serving dish and sprinkle with pitted olives, chopped onions, and fennel. Before serving, spoon the well-mixed dressing over them and add a few bits of the fennel leaves.

† *JAM ROLL PUDDING*

JAM ROLL	**CUSTARD**
2 egg yolks	3 eggs
6 tbsp sugar	4 tbsp sugar
2 tsp water	⅛ tsp salt
2 tsp lemon juice	2 cups scalded milk
½ cup cake flour	1 tsp vanilla
¾ tsp baking powder	
⅛ tsp salt	
2 egg whites, beaten stiff	
strawberry or apricot jam	

Preheat the oven to 400° F. Line a 6″ x 12″ baking sheet with wax paper and butter it well. Beat the egg yolks until thick. Still beating, add the sugar, water, and lemon juice. Combine the dry ingredients and beat the egg whites until stiff but not dry. Fold the dry ingredients and the egg whites alternately into the egg yolk mixture. When blended, spread the mixture on the baking sheet and bake 8 minutes.

Turn the cake upside down onto a dampened towel. Quickly cut away the edges using a long sharp knife or kitchen scissors. Roll the cake up with the towel and cool 10 minutes. Unroll and spread generously with strawberry or apricot jam. Reroll without the towel and let cool.

Make the custard by beating the eggs, sugar, and salt until thoroughly blended. Add the scalded milk gradually, still beating. Flavor with vanilla. Cook over very low heat, stirring until the mixture thickens enough to coat a spoon. Cool, stirring occasionally.

Slice the jam roll and line the bottom and sides of a glass dessert dish with the slices. Pour in a little custard and put in more of the roll. Repeat the process until both the custard and jam roll are used up, ending with a thin film of custard on the top. Chill in the refrigerator. This may be served plain, or with sweetened whipped cream.

† BRANDY SNAP ROLLS

¼ lb butter	juice of ½ lemon
½ cup sugar	1¼ cups heavy cream, whipped
6 tbsp dark corn syrup	with
1 cup flour	$\frac{1}{3}$ cup confectioners' sugar
⅛ tsp salt	and
1 tsp ground ginger	2 tbsp brandy

Preheat the oven to 350° F.

Melt the butter and add the sugar and syrup to it, stirring until blended. Remove from the heat. Combine the flour, salt, ginger, and lemon juice. Add to the butter and sugar mixture and stir well.

Butter a baking sheet and drop teaspoons of the mixture on the sheet, far enough apart to permit the cookies to spread. Bake 5 or 6 minutes or until golden brown, Remove from the oven and cool for 2 minutes. Loosen a cookie from the pan with a strong spatula, and quickly roll it around the thick handle of a wooden spoon. Slip the roll off and repeat the process. If the cookies become too brittle to roll, put them back in the oven for a moment. Cool the cookies and store in a covered cookie jar.

Just before serving, pipe the sweetened and flavored whipped cream into the rolls at each end, using a pastry bag with a cannelated tip. Allowing for a few misses, this recipe should make 24 filled rolls.

† *LEMON PANCAKES WITH SUMMER SAUCE*

PANCAKES
2 eggs
1 cup all-purpose flour
1¼ cups nonfat milk
½ tsp salt
1 tbsp brandy

FROSTING
3 tbsp butter
3 tbsp confectioners' sugar
2 tbsp lemon juice

SUMMER SAUCE
1 pint raspberries, strawberries, or blueberries
1 cup heavy cream, whipped with
¼ cup of confectioners' sugar and
1 tsp vanilla

Beat the eggs until foamy. Add the rest of the pancake ingredients and beat until smooth. The batter should be thin. Let it stand for at least an hour before using. Make thin 4 inch pancakes by frying them in lightly buttered crêpe pans, or, lacking these, in a skillet. Cook about 1 minute on each side. Roll the pancakes up and place them in a buttered heatproof serving dish.

For the frosting, mix the butter, sugar, and lemon juice into a paste, and spread on the top of each rolled pancake.

Just before serving, place the dish in a 500° F oven for about 5 minutes. Serve hot with the sauce made by combining the fruit or a mixture of fruit with the sweetened and flavored whipped cream. If fresh fruit is not available, thaw frozen fruit, pouring off most of the syrup, and reduce the amount of sugar in the whipped cream.

Murder
on the
Town

TWENTY-NINE

Londontown

The first essential value of the detective story lies in this, that it is the earliest and only form of popular literature in which is expressed some sense of the poetry of modern life. . . . Of this realization a great city itself as something wild and obvious the detective story is certainly the *Iliad*.

G. K. Chesterton, "A Defence of Detective Stories"

Big Ben strikes six-thirty. On the Embankment, people hurry and queue up for the top-heavy scarlet buses that stagger to a stop for a moment, gather a streamer of people and, with the dinging of a tiny bell, lumber off once more into the dusk. Something is about to happen.

Though the rain and fog heighten the sense of isolation, of pending or accomplished disaster, though the black water of the Thames underscores the perilous quality of city life, and all the elements participate, it is the city, not nature that creates the atmosphere of threat. The dark, bending trees which, in the country, signal the approach of something sinister, give way to chimney pots silhouetted against the darkening sky. The howling wind becomes the whine of traffic or the muted thunder of the Underground, pounding brutally and irrevocably toward us, while we stand shivering, feeling almost in its path. The hiss of tires becomes the sound of waves; omnibuses, the ships at sea. The current rushes in the thousands of people coming down Oxford Street, feeding the ducks in St. James's Park, catching trains at Victoria Station. In the city, the ambiguous menace of nature, lashing out as witlessly as a giant waking from slumber, takes on the imprint of man. *His* footsteps echo on the pavement, *his* car slows ominously to a stop on a silent, rain-slicked street, *his* looming buildings are carved with hidden passageways where something unknown lurks. Thus, London rules and conquers the mystery book.

In the urban mystery, the fear of nature is replaced by mistrust of the city, and the potential evil in man. The natural symbol for anxiety, the vague uneasiness at the sound of thunder, becomes the narrower, more personal fear of accident or violence. It is not rain but robbery we fear; not lightning but larceny. There is violence in the city, brutality is endemic, a corpse on the pavement is a shock, but it is not as out of place as the corpse in the copse or on the hearthrug.

The possibility of evil is everywhere. There is no idea that society is innocent: its members are unknown. In the city, the types of characters are the least confined of all the mystery book settings. They may be from all walks of life; their actions not predictable. Their families may have lived here for centuries, or they may have arrived on the train yesterday. Gone is the closed society of the village, its innocence broken in on by one uniquely guilty act, a single being who moves in relief against the stationary background. Neither the setting nor the society of the city is static. Everything is in motion; the eye must struggle to pick out the single figure lost in the many, to isolate accomplished from merely possible evil.

Vanished is the natural idyll, the harmonious quiet of the country; its undulant green, the distant roar of the sea, or the nearby dappling of a brook. Soothing horizontals are replaced by jarring verticals. A scream doesn't pierce serenity, it is lost in the squeal of brakes; a shot doesn't ring down the peace, it is unheard in the welter of automobile horns. The criminal may use the city to run, making its complexities his shield, its anonymities his means of escape.

The response of conscience, the pressure of goodness are taken over by the law. Enclosed society's unwritten laws, its standards, manners, customs, are replaced by the formal restraints and fear of the law. The criminal no longer confronts ostracism from his community, the implicit force of conformity. He runs against the explicit threat of retribution by an anonymous society's anonymous protectors. The would-be criminal no longer balances his need for the respect or well-wishes of those he knows with his aggressive impulses. Here, fear, a negative force—the eye for an eye—restrains him. Only the small, homogeneous, stable community can truly rule itself by common consent. The larger and more polyglot the community, the greater the threat of conflict and violence, the more force will answer force.

THIRTY

The Urban Police

In a social sense the detective story expresses in an extreme form the desire of the middle and upper classes in British society for a firm, almost hierarchical, social order, and for an efficient police force.

JULIAN SYMONS, "The Detective Story in Britain"

To counteract the rapacious animal the city produced and sheltered in its unwitting walls, a creature too inclined to roam free and maraud at its pleasure, the police force arose.

Prior to 1828, according to the Royal Commission on the Police, 1962: "Parliament seems to have feared less the visible dangers of insecurity . . . than the threat to liberty which it saw in an effective police force." As the city became more and more the victim of the rapid growth of population that followed the Industrial Revolution, it was slowly borne in on the most jealous libertarians that lawlessness could not be checked simply by increasingly severe penalties. In response to this awareness, in

1829 the Metropolitan Police Act provided for the organization of a united police force throughout London, except for the City, whose police to this day are under the control of municipal authorities. Ten years later, the County Police Act enabled justices to set up and maintain police forces in the counties. Both acts preserved the constable's common law powers, and his subordination to the justices. Under common law, the constable's powers make him an independent holder of a public office and, as such, an agent of the law of the land, not of the police authority or of the central government. Although his chief officer is liable for any wrongful act he commits in the performance of his duty, he himself is directly responsible, and can be sued.

According to "The Police Service in Britain," issued by the British Information Services: ". . . the limitations on their powers and their lack of firearms, the sanction of the police in enforcing the law rests, and must rest, in Great Britain, upon common consent—the basic conception of the police service being that its members are there to serve the public which they represent and to receive assistance from the public they serve."

In Dorothy Sayers's introduction to *Great Short Stories of Detection, Mystery and Horror,* she asserts there must be a sympathy for law and order for the mystery story to come into being, and that the reason for the mystery's popularity in England has to do with the Anglo-Saxon respect for the policeman as the law's representative. Other writers, Julian Symons among them, have pointed out that when the form arose, "in the latter part of the nineteenth century, its increasing popularity ran parallel to the development of the police force in Britain . . ."

In the mystery, the police act as the means of enforcement of the status quo. As representatives of the social order and the law that reflects it, they are empowered to keep things as they are. And they are as enthusiastic about the established order as anyone else. Talking with Chief Detective-Inspector Alleyn, of aristocrats and Macbeth, a constable in *Death of a Peer* proves a deep-dyed supporter of things as they are. The young man sums up his speculation with the observation that "You don't *expect* people of their class to commit murder."

The belief is so generally agreed upon, the gentleness of order so basic, the reins so lightly held in a society on the honor system, that the police go unarmed on the understanding that everyone wants fair play. The strongest force is mild disapproval. Law does not uphold order, tradition does. Law only hooks up the black sheep.

The instinct for sportsmanship and fair play is so great it reduces other scruples to also-rans. Even cardinal sins come in second. Father Ronald Knox, a mystery writer himself, in discussing the rules of fair play between mystery author and reader says they are not like the rules of poetry, but the rules of cricket, "a far more impressive consideration to the ordinary Englishman."

It is this tradition of sportsmanship in the legal code, says Dorothy Sayers, that gives the quarry sufficient rope to "provide a ding-dong chase."

THIRTY-ONE

The
Professional Policeman:
To the Manor Born

... the writer whose detective is a member of the official force has an advantage: from him a detached attitude is correct; he can suitably retain the impersonal attitude of a surgeon.

DOROTHY L. SAYERS, introduction to *Great Short Stories of Detection, Mystery and Horror*

For an essential difference between professional policeman and the aristocratic dabbler, one need go no further than the feet. Aristocratic detectives such as Campion and Wimsey barely bend the dandelions, leaving elfin impressions of lightly molded shoes, narrow, slightly pointed. Ngaio Marsh's Inspector Alleyn and Michael Innes's Inspector Appleby, on the other hand, assuredly wear stout size nine boots, and leave marks of a firm tread. Also, they have jaws. Not quite as jutting as American ones, perhaps, but jaws just the same. And substance. A probing finger would probably encounter solid flesh. Moreover, their voices are the same confident, secure, manly sounds that tell us at ten thousand feet we are about to crash.

The Professional Policeman: To the Manor Born † 199

Both Appleby and Alleyn are hybrid breeds. Though professional policemen, they are gentlemen, despite the worthy housekeeper's opinion given to a flighty maid in Miss Sayers's *The Unpleasantness at the Bellona Club:* ". . . gentleman-like I will not deny, but a policeman is a person, and I will trouble you to remember it."

As gentlemen, Appleby's and Alleyn's manners are polished. They carry their pipes and their tweeds well. They drop literary allusions and witticisms. They know their food and wine. In short, they are perfectly nice, sensible, God-is-my-co-pilot men, pleasant to encounter, not one irritating mannerism or attitude between them. Though it would be possible to get into a rather heated argument about Poirot and Wimsey—as heated as if they were flesh-and-blood creatures capable of choice and action—it would be a strain to have a difference of opinion about Appleby or Alleyn.

Almost none of the police detectives are lone wolves. All are happily married, or become so in the course of their adventures, while their children, like most children in mystery books, are generally kept away. Murder is bad for children; it is better to have them upstairs with Nanny, neither heard nor seen, neither hearing nor seeing. Screams in the night give children nightmares and traumas; funny food can turn their little minds. Children cause worry in readers, particularly women. Why hasn't Peter been put to bed? When will Rose have her tea, etc. Better for them to read about Dad in the Sunday supplements where he appears with the regularity of a film star. The police detective in England is as familiar as a soccer hero to the nation at large. Not only is his name known; he is immediately recognizable in the heart of fen country or at a Panda crossing in London.

In his need to be detached, the police detective must look on crime almost unfeelingly or risk, as would a physician, a clouding of his efficiency and objectivity. Feelings, and a too-active imagination, only get in his way. In the process, as he knows to his pain, he finds himself dehumanized. Innes's Inspector Cadover or Josephine Tey's Inspector Grant are frequently overcome with a sense of isolation and self-disgust for the role their work makes them play vis-á-vis their fellow men.

There can be nothing frivolous about the police detective; he is, after all, a public servant and, as such, must take his job seriously. He is primarily a reasoning machine, a collector of clues, a patient pursuer of information great or small. In his preface to *Tales of Crime and Detection*, E. M. Wrong says, "A detective cannot flourish till there is methodical criminal procedure requiring proof."

Instead of the deft, gay turns, and agile leaps of intuition afforded the aristocratic detective, the average police detective is constricted to a life of service without embellishment. His superiority is not a matter of breeding. He has "beaten" his way up, risen from the ranks on the arches of his flattened feet and the backbone of solid, middle-class virtues. He excels by dint of effort, and steadfastness, not primarily by dazzling insights. He gives evidence of a struggle; it is possible he will even sweat. Possible, but not likely. The very neutrality, the mechanical methodology, however, that makes it possible for him to look on a crime with almost inhuman objectivity, to be surgical and detached without being callous, have also made him distinctly dull. 'Tis sad but true, the most memorable of the established characters in detective fiction come the closest to being annoying, and the least memorable are the most ordinary. Even Dorothy Sayers has to admit that Lord Peter Wimsey annoys almost everyone but Inspector Parker, and his man, Bunter, allows that the "liveliness" of his lordship's manner could give offense to the unimaginative. But having read, one does not forget him. On the other hand, professional policemen, with not one distinguishing mannerism among them, are almost wholly interchangeable, therefore completely forgettable.

From the outset of detective fiction writing, the trick has been to create detectives of enough interest, yet void of distracting emotions to weaken their objectivity and detachment.

Gradually, to make their detectives more "real," writers began to reduce the number and strength of idiosyncrasies. The characters did not, however, become proportionately more real. Just as idiosyncrasies did not make characters real, neither did their absence. The problem seems to have been a confusion of "real" with "bland." Hercule Poirot's characteristics are exaggerated, unleavened by subtlety, but there are nuggets of truth secreted in both his behavior and his observations. The same is true to an even greater extent of Miss Marple. Miss Marple is, like all Miss Christie's characters, a stereotype, but as Miss Marple herself is so fond of pointing out, "Human nature is much the same anywhere." There are really very few types of people in the world.

Poirot might be likened to a stuffed duck in a toy store, as opposed to Josephine Tey's Inspector Grant, who would then be likened to a decoy sitting on a pond. Of the two, the decoy appears more real to the eye, but if examined closely, it would be found, in other respects, no more like a living duck than the toy in the shop. Poirot may be a caricature, but a caricature necessarily resembles something actual. Even Inspector Grant's ill health and claustrophobia make only one side of him more real, as if we colored one eye of a cardboard figure blue. By resembling everyone, the police detective resembles no one and nothing at all; just as the absorption of all light is black, of all numbers is a neuter. By making him superman, he becomes no-man.

The result of the personality vacuum is that fools rush in in droves; the supporting players steal the show; the spoon runs away with the dish. Appleby, whose wit raises him a notch above the rest of the police detectives is, even so, little more than a dead center: the pole of the maypole dance, the support of the carnival tent, the landing strip for the flights of fantasy, the straight man for the ramshackle ribaldries of his in-laws, the Ravens. That Innes can succeed at combining fantasy with the detective story is clear from the beautifully Alice-in-Wonderland passage on the circus train in *The Case of the Journeying Boy,* and the superbly humorous rendering of the elder Bolderwood's trials with his misbegotten staff in the same book. Frequently, however, the Ravens might be just running by on their way to Stella Gibbons's *Cold Comfort Farm*—itself a quasi-Brontë would of throbbing over- and undertones by way of Li'l Abner—but a work meritoriously concentrated on being solely fantastic satire. For Innes, Appleby becomes the knife that cuts the butter, the slice of sanity in an ocean of whimsy and hyperactive wit.

Level-headed Inspector Alleyn, in Ngaio Marsh's *Death of a Peer,* fades before the elegances of the eccentricity-proud Lamprey family. Even when the hero is not part of the jut-jawed school of detection, and is himself eccentric, he may be given, as the paler-than-Wimsey Campion is, a run for his money by, in his case, his man Lugg. Miss Allingham's Lugg is the polar opposite of Wimsey's gentlemanly gentleman's gentleman, Bunter, but he is equally unforgettable.

While Campion tunes his inner ear to foolish ditties from undergraduate days, Lugg launches into limey language like a capering behemoth. His emotions are prehensile, his feelings are tender and virginal in the manner of the prostitute with the heart of gold. Called "friend and knave" by Campion, the stalwart oaf doesn't know his place; he is the butt of a hundred incidents in which he plays the fool in what is meant, presumably, to be the Shakespearean manner.

The principal function of the detective's "leftenant," be he his man or inspector, is to give us access to the detective's thinking, to give us an insight into his omniscience. But as his foil, he distinguishes the detective by contrast. If the detective is will-o'-the-wisp as Campion, the leftenant is massive and unrefined as Lugg; if ingenious as Poirot, ingenuous as Hastings; if as full of aristocratic flair as Wimsey, as methodically middle class as Inspector Parker. In some cases, by the sharpness of contrast alone, the leftenant furnishes comic relief. Without the restrictions placed on the detective, their partners-in-crime are allowed infinitely more license in personality. But they must, however bumptious or suave their exterior, give tacit recognition to the superiority of the detective and their unquestioning loyalty, and however obstreperously unconventional they appear, the partners-in-crime must be moral, and support the detective in his social mission. For his part, the detective will boldly and bravely earn this loyalty and support, at whatever cost to his personality and interest, by submerging his individuality for the common good. He simply *cannot* have too good a time.

THIRTY-TWO

The Mixed Palette

"... the doctor's story is not going to be obvious. Far from it. . . . But I observe the waiter hovering uneasily about us while his colleagues pile up chairs and carry away the cruets. Will you not come and finish the story in my flat? I can give you a glass of very decent port."

DOROTHY L. SAYERS, *Unnatural Death*

Within the great glow of London is the smaller, exciting glitter of Soho with its ring of restaurants, Chinamen, and rough, unsavory traffic. Soho is nothing but restaurants. Doorway after doorway beckoning, menu after menu winking behind the glass. Taxis drive up to deposit theatergoers coming for late supper. While gentlemen go to their clubs, and spinsters to the Army and Navy Stores to keep the flow of British cuisine to their vitals unimpeded, the adventuresome, the sophisticates, try the dishes that Cook cannot provide.

The most cosmopolitan city in the world reflects its days of empire, the multiplicity of its citizenry and visitors by offering the widest selection of cuisines in the greatest number of restaurants: Greek, Indian, Italian, French, Hungarian, Pekinese—

delicious, inviting. Nightclubs tucked here and there hold out the dimness and privacy so necessary to a police-inspector keeping watch behind a decaying palm for a regular patron; the flow of alcohol essential to the aristocratic detective, soothing out a story, or a vital piece of information; the lobster and champagne required by a young man about town trying to impress a femme fatale, or the orchestra to dance to with a Flighty Deb; a place where a lovely woman can be discreetly murdered when the lights go down before the drums of the dance band roll; or a band man may be stabbed as the cymbals clash. A restaurant is very accommodating.

Restaurants and nightclubs have exotic names and Italian waiters. Hercule Poirot may be called to a party at one of the tables, celebrating the anniversary of one murder with another. Some restaurants have entertainment, as well.

If the detective is not already seated at the table where the murder takes place, he can be quickly located at one not too far away—on one of his rare nights out on the tiles—in the traditional is-there-a-doctor-in-the-house manner. After the nightclub closes, he will round up all the waiters and members of the band, and question them amidst upturned chairs and bare tables.

The turbulent artist's life is lived in Chelsea. Glamorous actors and actresses, working like a carnival troupe or a pack of gypsies, suffering excesses of nonfeeling and fame, are a magnet for the wealthy idler, the aristocratic detective, and the police inspector. All around is mayhem. Artists kill each other off at an alarming rate. Of course, it does raise the value of their works. Living overlong, like being prolific, can be death to an artist.

In Chelsea, people go from party to party in studios in the mews, eating caviar with pickle forks, cutting their way through kippers and sausages to listen to a poet reading his latest verse, or to see the most recent enormity of a sculptor. If ever a *crime passionel* occurs, it is here, where tempers run high, and morals are loose, where Bolshevism and free love mix and meet around the samovar in smoke-filled rooms, while chic and rich young women attempt to rub off some of the moth-wing glamour on themselves.

Part of the excitement, and well worth the hazards, are the opportunities in these districts to loosen the palate along with the morals. Forgotten, for the moment, the wholesome sanity and sturdy cooking of a country background, as one dreamily lifts another forkful of food redolent of faraway places, and thinks avant-garde thoughts.

EXOTICA AND SAVORIES
Gratinéed Oysters
Vitello Tonnato
Pilaf with Curried Mussels
Breast of Lamb, Indian Style
Indian Tandoori Chicken
Jugged Hare
Stuffed Mussels

† *GRATINÉED OYSTERS*
(4 servings)

24 large oysters
½ pint heavy cream
1 tsp grated, bottled horseradish

3 tbsp grated Parmesan
   cheese
3 tbsp melted butter
cayenne

Open the oysters and cut them loose from the shells, leaving them in the deeper half shells. Mix the cream and horseradish, and put 2 tsp on each oyster. Sprinkle with the Parmesan cheese and dribble the butter over them. Put a tiny bit of cayenne on each. Broil for 5 minutes. Serve immediately, allowing 6 per person.

† VITELLO TONNATO
(8 to 10 servings)

3 to 4 lb boned leg of veal roast	2 tsp salt
1 carrot, sliced	6 peppercorns
1 onion, sliced	7-oz can tuna fish
2 celery stalks, sliced	2 tsp anchovy paste
1 bay leaf	2 tbsp lemon juice
¼ tsp powdered thyme	½ cup olive oil
2 cups dry white wine	salt and black pepper
2 cups water	1 tbsp capers
	chopped parsley

Place the meat, which should be firmly tied, in a kettle with the vegetables, herbs, wine, water, salt and peppercorns. Bring to a boil. Cover tightly and cook slowly for 2½ to 3 hours. Remove the meat from the kettle and put in a bread pan or other suitable container. Cover with another bread pan and weight it down with some heavy object. Cool, and then place in the refrigerator. Boil down the liquid in the kettle until it measures about 1 cup. Strain and cool.

Put the tuna fish, anchovy paste, lemon juice, and one cup of the liquid in a blender. Spin to a purée, gradually adding the olive oil. Season with salt and black pepper. Cut the veal in thin slices and lay them on a large platter. Cover with the tuna sauce and sprinkle with the capers and chopped parsley. Serve with Italian bread.

† PILAF WITH CURRIED MUSSELS
(4 servings)

2 quarts mussels	2 tbsp flour
2 cups dry white wine	1 tsp curry powder
½ bay leaf	½ pint medium cream
4 sprigs parsley	chopped parsley
5 tbsp butter	fresh or frozen peas
1 large onion, chopped fine	
1½ cups long grain rice	

Put thoroughly washed and scraped mussels in a kettle with the wine and herbs. Cover tightly and cook over a high heat until the mussels open. Cool enough to handle. Remove the mussels from the shells and put them in a bowl. Strain the broth through a strainer lined with cheesecloth.

Heat 3 tbsp butter in a skillet and cook the onion and rice until the onion is soft and the rice transparent. Measure 3½ cups of mussel broth and add ½ cup of boiling water. Add ½ cup of this liquid to the rice, and when that is absorbed add more liquid until 2½ cups have been absorbed. When the rice is just tender it is ready.

Meanwhile heat 2 tbsp butter in a saucepan. Stir in the flour and curry powder and let it brown lightly. Stir in the remaining 1½ cups of diluted mussel broth and stir until smooth. Add the mussels and the cream. Reheat but do not boil.

Place the rice in a heated dish and sprinkle with chopped parsley. Surround with freshly cooked fresh or frozen peas. Serve the curried mussels in a companion dish.

† BREAST OF LAMB, INDIAN STYLE
(4 to 6 servings)

2½ lbs breast of lamb	3 tbsp butter
3 onions	4 cardamom seeds
2 cloves garlic	½ cup ground almonds
½ cup yogurt	2 tsp salt
1 tsp ground ginger	⅛ tsp saffron *or*
¼ tsp cinnamon	2 tsp turmeric
pinch each of ground cloves	½ cup heavy cream
and cardamom	chopped parsley

Trim the lamb and cut it into ¾ inch cubes. Place them in a non-metallic bowl. Slice the onions fine. Measure and put half of them in a blender with the garlic, yogurt, and spices. Spin to a purée and mix with the lamb. Let stand at least 30 minutes.

Heat the butter in a skillet and brown the remaining onions with the cardamom seeds over a moderate heat. Add the meat mixture and stir over high heat for 10 minutes, stirring constantly. Stir in the almonds and the salt. Cover and simmer for 45 minutes. Add the saffron or, lacking that, the turmeric mixed with water. Continue cooking for 15 minutes.

Place the mixture in a heated serving dish. Cover with heavy cream and serve with chutney and Fluffy Rice (see page 260). Sprinkle with chopped parsley.

† INDIAN TANDOORI CHICKEN
(8 servings)

Tandoori mix is found in stores that provide staples for international cooking.

2 3½ lb fryers, quartered	salt
¼ lb butter	1 tbsp lime or lemon juice
½ cup Tandoori mix	onion rings (raw or fried, canned
1 cup yogurt	or frozen)

Skin the chicken pieces, using a sharp knife to cut the skin away from the bones and to detach the filaments that attach the skin to the flesh.

Heat the butter and stir in the Tandoori mix. Remove from the heat and stir in the yogurt. Line a roasting pan with aluminum foil and place the chicken pieces in it, flesh side up. Sprinkle with salt and coat with the yogurt mixture. Let stand 3 to 4 hours or overnight.

Cover with foil and bake 40 minutes at 400° F. Remove the foil and bake 10 minutes longer. Place the quarters on a heated platter and pour the sauce from the pan over them. Sprinkle with the lime or lemon juice and a little salt. Garnish with the onion rings and serve with Fluffy Rice (see page 260), and an avocado and lettuce salad. A cold sherbet is very refreshing after the spiciness of this dish.

† JUGGED HARE
(6 servings)

Here we have to substitute, since hare is not easy to come by. Frozen rabbit, however, is in nationwide supermarkets and can make a very tasty dish.

4 to 5 lb frozen rabbit	1 lemon, sliced
¾ cup red burgundy	bouquet garni (parsley, bay leaf,
4 tbsp olive oil	tied)
1 small onion, sliced	¼ tsp thyme
4 to 6 juniper berries, crushed	½ tsp salt
flour	canned bouillon
2 large onions	2 tbsp butter
2 cloves	3 tbsp flour

Thaw the rabbit and cut into small chunks. Place them in a non-metallic bowl and marinate them in the wine, olive oil, onion, and juniper berries for 4 to 6 hours, stirring occasionally so that each piece gets well coated. Remove from the marinade and wipe dry. Dust with flour.

Heat the butter in a skillet and brown the rabbit pieces well. Preheat the oven to 375° F. Place the browned rabbit pieces in a deep casserole, known in this recipe as a jug. Pack them in tightly. Add the onions stuck with the cloves, the lemon slices, and the bouquet garni tied in a piece of cheesecloth. Add the thyme and salt. Strain the marinade into the casserole, and add enough hot bouillon to cover the meat. Cover tightly and bake 3 hours. Remove the rabbit from the casserole and discard the bouquet.

Strain the gravy into a sauce pan. Bring it to a boil, adding a paste made of butter and flour bit by bit as you stir. When the sauce is smooth and thick, put the rabbit back in the casserole and pour the sauce over it. Wrap the casserole prettily with a white napkin and serve with red currant jelly, white beans, and a tossed green salad.

† *STUFFED MUSSELS*
(6 to 8 servings)

48 mussels	TOPPING
¼ lb butter	4 medium potatoes
2 large cloves garlic, pressed	2 tbsp butter
2 tbsp chopped parsley	2 eggs
2 tbsp dry vermouth	1 egg yolk

Scrape and scrub the mussels and put them in a kettle with a cup of water. Cover tightly and let them steam until they open, for about 10 minutes. Remove from the heat and let cool until they can be handled. Take off the top shell from each, and place the shell with the mussel in it on a baking dish.

Make a paste of the butter, garlic, parsley, and vermouth. Dot each mussel with the paste.

Peel and boil the potatoes in salted water. Force through a food mill or potato ricer. Mix in the butter, the slightly beaten eggs and egg yolk, salt, and pepper. Beat until fluffy. Cover each mussel with the potato mixture, using a knife or piping it through a pastry bag.

Five minutes before serving put the mussels under a preheated broiler, and broil until golden brown.

THIRTY-THREE

The
Aristocratic Detective:
An Embarrassment
of Riches

There are so many ways in which a gentleman should be unnoticeable.

MICHAEL INNES, *The Case of the Journeying Boy*

The genealogy of aristocratic detectives is so awe-inspiring it is best kept secret. Too overwhelming. Readers picking themselves up from the floor. "Did you know that Wimsey . . . Alfred the Gr— . . . Duke of Well—. . ." Thud. Too, too much. To protect the living, the detectives' origins and antecedents are frequently treated to the coy obliqueness of dates and place names in nineteenth-century novels. "In 18— in the town of Br—— in the province of V——— in southern France," etc. The result of even so guarded a reference will mean an extra lot of stammers and blushes for Margery Allingham's Albert Campion, and another bout of foolishness for Dorothy Sayers's Lord Peter Wimsey. Poor chaps. It is best to remember, fitfully, with Miss Harriet Vane, that Wimsey is Somebody, and let it go at that. The thing to do is to live it down.

Living it down is a lifetime occupation. Fortunately, His Lordship will have the whole team rooting for him. Nanny, for starters. Nanny will see to it that your ego never rises above the nursery table. The English public school, to which you will be sent the first moment your parents might become attached to you, is guaranteed to knock it out of you. A lifetime of being hazed. Self-indulgence, solidly trounced. The ego, repositioned at the bottom of the boot, toughened to leather, till all that remains is discipline stripped so bare it is little more than animal pride at survival. After such a youth, life's giant arenas become jolly as a game of tiddlywinks, M.P., P.M., B.B.C. Easy as pie. To those who come through the harshnesses of public school, the realities of this world offer no threats.

As a result of these strenuous efforts to shape him, the aristocrat is an expert in frivolity. He can make light of anything that could conceivably have its root in privilege. His, the hard-earned dilettante's disguise that will help him be taken lightly, not as a serious pursuer of crime; the flair not given and not allowed to his professional confreres. If one involves himself in philanthropy, for example, he must joke about it. Philanthropy, duty, service are, after all, luxuries. The poor have neither time nor money for them. His knowledge of languages? Anyone could. The butler's is better. A family of nodding coronets? "I don't know if they'd interest you, darling. Quite a tedious lot, really, though Mama is a good nut. That tumbling pile? Oh, yes, the lawns are quite good. Capability Brown's, y'know." Life is little more than a prolonged excuse for scuffing one's toe in the dust, murmuring, "It's nothing."

In some cases, making light of oneself goes so far pigment and even ectoplasm drain away. Albert Campion was
originally fey as one of Topper's cronies. His hair was colorless,
as were his virtually sightless eyes. The war put some starch
in him. Lord Peter Wimsey is so thin that when he climbs a
drainpipe the only way you can tell which is which is that one
moves.

Even the brain seems to be affected. Like the country
gentleman, the aristocratic detective is honor bound to appear
ineffectual, if not downright half-witted. The vacant gaze of
Wimsey, the pale brows of Campion, are the end results of a long
tradition, endemic to the breed as long fingernails to the mandarin. The mandarin never lifted his hands to work; the gentleman never lowers his mind to the material. This deliberate
wresting of the gaze from the here and now has had the curious
side effect of fogging the vision altogether. Hence, pince-nez
and monocle.

These weaknesses, however, are not a bone to be tossed to
the lower classes to give them something to feel superior about.
As with the eccentricity, i.e., advanced nonworldliness, of the
upper class, they are meant to be wholly admirable traits. Even
the seeming foolishness is meant only to heighten the contrast
between the deft workings of a clever brain and a simple exterior; and gives the simpleton in us all a chance to thumb our
noses at the slickies. The poverty of appearance—like the material poverty of that American phoenix, the boy who rises from
rags to riches—is merely the external weakness of a wet destined
for heroism; a lad who will run from the cricket fields to the
glories of war. When duty calls, every little birch-beaten back
stiffens to its command. When the scarlet banner of crime
waves, the seemingly ineffectual young man shows a wrist of
steel.

So the weed at Eton rises, eyes shining sightlessly behind

thick glasses, spindly knees knocking under spindly trousers, to take over the reins of government or, as a detective, the wheel of a Daimler-Six. Both are forms of service, the one luxury the rich can afford to enjoy. Using his Oxford-trained brain, the aristocratic detective is free to track his quarry with a ruthlessness to match the murderer's own. Without murder, the same detective, with his first folios, fine wines, and profitless erudition, would be one tottering step from decadence. With it, he may wholeheartedly relish the mixture of duty—the counterweight of privilege—and pleasure. Everything in his background has equipped him, made him the White Knight to fight the dragon, the threat to society. As befits a member of the landed gentry, he tills the fields of the mind, but most important, he hunts.

THIRTY-FOUR

Lord Peter Wimsey: The Moment Wimsicale

... a well-made road, a lively engine and the prospect of a good corpse at the end of it, Lord Peter's cup of happiness was full. He was a man who loved simple pleasures.

DOROTHY L. SAYERS, *Five Red Herrings*

Oh, what is so rare as a day in August with a good car, and a corpse waiting, tangled in the weir? Joyous and babbling, his pleasure at murder undisguised, Wimsey is the epitome of the aristocratic detective. His, the embarrassing riches, the aged titles, the requisite idiocy, the tossaway virtue of the nobleman.

Second son of the 15th Duke of Denver, Wimsey's aristocratic birth is clear from his pallor, his monocle, and a tendency to burst out with such resonantly virile cries as "cheerfully-righty-o" and powerful affirmatives as "absobally-lutely positive." If so unsubstantial a being can be said to have specifics—he is slight, he is fair, he is myopic.

Biographical details are furnished, with crest and motto, at the beginning of *Unnatural Death* by "his maternal uncle, Paul Delagardie." According to him, Wimsey is quite a decent chap, at bottom. He was saved by the bat from impending wetness at Eton; his cricket heroics are still recalled. For a while at Oxford he became a worry again. Showed signs of going all scholarly. He still bears traces. Mulling over a folio of Justinian, when he isn't playing Bach on the small grand piano. Dropping quotes from *Alice's Adventures in Wonderland*. Bally lad can't ask for a sandwich without calling out the White King for support. And, of course, there's liable to be Latin, as well. Still, when you consider what a near thing it was. . . .

To his uncle, Wimsey owes his taste for the finest, and to his family, the money to get it. His wines, his women, his songs are culled from the best. Chef and poisoner alike acknowledge his connoisseurship of food; an exclusive club hangs on his judgment of a wine; his lawyer avows he has the discrimination of a man twice his age; a young woman friend pays highest tribute of all, saying he doesn't talk rubbish about art, doesn't want his hand held, and his mind always turns on eating and drinking. Lobster and champagne make him shiver; a woman who turns them down is commended: "The moment I found she preferred burgundy to champagne I had the highest opinion of her." Wimsey is at home at the Savoy, where he orders with the sureness of an orchestra conductor arranging his effects: "*Huitres Musgraves*—I am opposed on principle to the cooking of oysters—but it is a dish so excellent that one may depart from the rules in its favor. Fried in their shells . . . with little strips of bacon. . . . The soup must be *Tortue Vraie*, of course. The fish— oh! just a *Filet de Sole*, the merest mouthful, a hyphen between the prologue and the main theme." The main theme is a *Faisan Roti, Pommes Byron*, and a "salad to promote digestion. And waiter, be sure the salad is dry and perfectly crisp. A *Soufflé Glacé* to finish up with."

The war left Lord Peter with two legacies: the first, a tendency to nervous collapses, now cleverly concealed beneath a dilettante's façade. With the blithering heroes of P. G. Wodehouse who, even in the prime of life, teeter, totter, or toddle along more often than they walk, Wimsey is inclined, when taking leave, to "make a noise like a hoop and roll away," or "like a bee and buzz off."

The second legacy is his sergeant, Bunter. Should one ever begin to suspect that the cards are all stacked in favor of the upper classes, he has only to consider Bunter. His Lordship's man is in many ways superior to his Lordship. Bunter's authority to snap up first folios in Wimsey's stead is ample tribute to Bunter's taste and cultivation. Wimsey's awe, and wistful hope of catching Bunter out in fatigue or failure, are proof of his strength and intelligence.

In deference to the English social system (a place for everyone, and everyone in his place), his man never takes advantage of this superiority. It would never cross his mind to challenge the right of the fair head and myopic eyes of His Lordship to rule. That comes with short pants, schooling at Eton, and privilege as heavy as a milestone. On the contrary, Bunter neither allows Lord Peter democracy toward himself nor others. When, in *Clouds of Witness*, Lord Peter refers to a young woman as a "young lady," Bunter responds, "I found the young person" ("Snubbed again," mutter[s] Lord Peter) "perfectly amiable, my lord . . ." Offered Wimsey's outstretched hand in fellowship, Bunter pretends not to see it. And, when he attempts to thank Bunter for saving his life, nearly at the expense of his own, Lord Peter winds up apologizing for his gaucherie with, "All right, I won't be embarrassin' or anything—thanks awfully, anyhow"! It is entirely probable that the English gentleman learns his most prized trait, detachment, from his man, rather than the reverse.

No, it is in the very obviousness of their superiority that

the Bunters of life show their want of breeding. The difference between shine and patina on silver. *Noblesse oblige* and *honi soit qui mal y pense*. Also, a partridge in a pear tree. Bunter is as dryly humorous and intelligent as any gentleman but, unfortunately, he is also as competent, capable, and down to earth as no gentleman would ever be. Though he is superior, Bunter is not upper class.

It is Bunter's privilege to serve; to second Wimsey, and enlarge his scope. While Wimsey thinks in rhyme, Bunter marks the meter. While Wimsey dashes, Bunter is prosaic. But though Bunter serves, he is not servile. Reflecting the knightly tradition from which they descend, Wimsey says in *The Unpleasantness at the Bellona Club*, "I believe Bunter would stick to me whatever happened. He was my N.C.O. during part of the War, and we went through some roughish bits together . . . I don't know what I should do without Bunter now."

Fortunately, he doesn't have to find out. No matter how assiduous his own pursuit of crime, Bunter still manages to keep the home fires burning. Everything runs like clockwork. Baths are drawn. Airs whistled. The morning *café au lait* is brought in, steaming in a Queen Anne coffee pot on a silver tray. Dust never settles. The harmony is never disturbed.

With Bunter's care, the Mayfair flat is as seductive a trap, and as peaceful a setting as can be imagined. The primrose-and-black walls of the sitting room are lined with tastefully decaying leatherbound books; first folios loom above. Here and there, a Piranesi drawing, a splash of parrot tulips. A fire glowing on the deep mahogany of piano and Chippendale chairs. The welcoming depths of a leather armchair, and a commodious chesterfield, heaped with fat silk cushions. Not a jarring note. It is concentrated luxury, distilled, like the ruby of the port; eminently enjoyable. The flat has always been there; it will always be there. The home of a purposeful dilettante; the place from which, revitalized, wits sharpened, Wimsey may spring yet again into the fray, secure in his ever-present man-at-arms, deftly discharging the tedious detail, happy to be what he is: a man who may not, and does not, aspire to more.

The Wimsey fortune is also accommodating enough to keep Lord Peter in a Daimler-Six called, in Dickensese, Mrs. Merdle. The slim black vehicle, powered with a racing motor, and shining with polished copper twin exhausts, is the speeding symbol of his wealth and dilettantism. It wheels him jovially and indiscriminately from corpse to copse for a picnic of crime.

But if his background of privilege provides both penchant and wherewithal for dilettantism, his support of the Cattery assuages his social conscience, while providing a service ready-made to spring into action when a bit of gossip-and-snoop is required for an investigation. Knitting gives the women entrée at vicarage working parties; typing provides the opening in an office where delicate wills are just a safecrack away; jingly chains at the neck and woolly jumpers give them easy access to essential boardinghouse chat, and companionable cups of tea. As an aristocrat, however, it is necessary that Wimsey belittle even his philanthropy.

Through Harriet Vane, we touch the subtle and melancholy strain in Wimsey's character. For her, the mask of foolishness falls completely away, the knight's armor glitters. But the damsel in distress will not be rescued.

Miss Vane is a woman Wimsey saved from a murder conviction to pursue indefatigably. He gets nothing in return for his pains but sour suspicion. In Wimsey's relationship with Miss Vane, the author, Miss Sayers, completely ignores her own warning that "a too violent emotion flung into the glittering mechanism of the detective-story jars the movement by distrubing its delicate balance." Involving Wimsey in a lingering love affair could have no other outcome than to triple his output of romantic allusions, send him punting down the Isis, and set him to accompanying himself on the spinet, while singing Elizabethan love lyrics. At its liveliest, Wimsey's and Harriet's courtship has the chuckling quality of two volumes of *Bartlett's*

Quotations tossing phrases at each other.

In his pursuit of crime, Wimsey is as indefatigable as in pursuit of love, and better rewarded. Wimsey's absurdities take on charm when used, not just as a shield, but as a weapon. The closer Wimsey comes to the solution of the crime, the sharper the contrast between dilettante and detective. The more intent he is, the more foolish he attempts to appear, growing sillier and slangier in inverse proportion to his seriousness, while his extralegal position allows a kind of fancifulness in action impossible to the police. He barges in, tactlessly questioning, with a kind of Blimpian, emotional short-sightedness which, though irritating, is liable to make his subjects more conscious of him than of his questions.

Mental muscles taut, ruthlessly using any weapon that comes to hand, he searches the unknown opponent with the witting and murderous accuracy of Hamlet stabbing Polonius behind the arras. He cheerfully pulls strings, orders the police about, sets Bunter on the trail, spends money with a lavish hand, answers craft with craft, dodge with dodge, furnishing a vigorous and insistent counterpoint to the criminal. All the privilege that has been his rises to his support: the wit-sharpening education, the eager, disciplined intellect untarnished by emotion, the indifference to self, the wealth that frees his mind and gives him easy passage, the power that opens doors, the indomitable spirit that will not be stopped. Wimsey, musician of murder, plays it with the unsentimental precision of a fugue, all stops pulled out, amusing himself with piccolos and grace notes until he sounds the final trumpet. Pity the poor wrongdoer!

THIRTY-FIVE

Hercule Poirot: Psychologist of Murder

"Then think, Hastings—*think.* Lie back in your chair, close the eyes, employ the little grey cells."

AGATHA CHRISTIE, *Poirot Loses a Client*

What does a Frency-tongued Belgian do when mired in England? He complains, *bien sur!* He complains, and assuages his sorrow with a sirop in the afternoon. Or a pot of chocolate in the morning. He complains, and remembers the Ritz. He weeps into watery soup served in a country inn for the sturdy pleasures of a pot-au-feu, then hurries back to his man, George, for I'm afraid, yes, an omelet prepared in a trice. Like all my-man's omelets, it is delicious. Hens just dropped by to lay the eggs; the butter is frothily fresh.

With such a continental gourmet stepping onto the pages,

the food level necessarily rises. *Pâté de foie gras* and toast offer themselves before a crackling fire. Sole surrounds itself in pale green grapes or sauces itself *à la Jeanette*. Omelets take on *fines herbes*. A meltingly tender *escalope de veau,* luxuriating in a sauce Milanese, loosens a lawyer's tongue, while a *poire flambée* glistens with ice cream; and a cool Pouilly Fuissé, a fragrant Corton, and a *crème de cacao* add their peerless drops. A dozen oysters, cheerfully seasoned with strychnine pave the way for artichoke soup, fish pie, and an apple tart. A meal on the Orient Express ends with a flourish of delicate cream cheese, and a liqueur. Yet, fear not, the sensible continental, Poirot, settles any misgivings a stomach might have for such flights with a bottle of mineral water.

From exclamations to parsimony, from egg-shaped head to patent-leather toe, there are a hundred ways in which Agatha Christie's detective, Poirot, signs himself Gaul.

Years in England have done nothing to deflate the little man—appearance, accent, or ego. All the tailors in Savile Row can't disguise the distinctiveness which M. Poirot is the first to admit, admire and, in fact, to keep as well polished as his patent leather boots. Far from melting into the scenery, he stands out in a crowd. He is the kind of man children point to, grown men nibble their mustaches to keep from laughing at, and strangers in a village never ask directions of. He is obviously funny and foreign.

Part of Poirot's foolishness is, of course, that he doesn't think he's ridiculous—far from it. One of his most un-English characteristics is the very seriousness with which he takes himself. As he would never laugh at himself, we laugh for him; which is the essence of being ridiculous. He is, in all, vain, conceited, and openly clever, a fact so immodestly revealed as to repel his English acquaintances.

If conceit is often a fault of murderers, it is rarely so of detectives. But Poirot is an exceptional man. His vanities and conceits are as extravagant as the luxuriant mustaches—whose tor-

tured splendor are variously and often described in the rhap-
sodic style due a Cyrano's nose—from which his vanity flows, as
Samson's strength from his hair.

He is a dandy, yes. But very much the Gallic dandy, bun-
dled against drafts on a midsummer's day in chic silk scarf and
fawn overcoat, spreading a handkerchief before sitting on a
damp rock, hidden in layers of coats and mufflers on a railway
platform in Turkey till only a pink nose and the waxed tips of
his mustaches show.

Not only do drafts have their usual fatal-to-Frenchmen
character for Poirot, they carry the added threat of twiddling his
mustaches. It is a fact, of course, that drafts pursue figure eights
to avoid Englishmen, who don't mind them, and rush with tor-
nado zest at the French, who hate them. Therefore, when riding
in an open car, Poirot holds his scarf like a Moslem woman's
veil, lest the wind trifle with the fierce virility of his mustaches'
waxed points. He would not travel without the spirit stove and
curling tongs for his mustache, and carries a tiny mirror in his
pocket.

The man behind the man, George, is as orderly as the
valet to such a man would have to be, and is every inch the English gentleman's gentleman: taciturn, competent, never giving
way to unseemly curiosity about the occasionally bizarre requests of his master. It is George who brings the pot of chocolate, who packs for a fortnight in the country and lays out Poirot's dress suit on arrival. It is George, too, who does his best
to capture Poirot's straying idioms.

Poirot's handling, or mishandling, of English is one of his
charms. It stands, in part, for the accent we cannot hear. He
can't use contractions, do not you understand? and uses "regard," "march," and "amiable" as if they were interchangeable
in both languages. He muddles his word order. He expresses
himself in a florid and un-English way: "There is a mouse in this
hole. What move must the cat make now?" or when his friend,
Captain Hastings, suggests a return to London after what he

considers a fruitless mission, Poirot retorts, "If you show the dog the rabbit, my friend, does he return to London?" In the early books, his lapses into French are translated in editor's notes at the bottom of the page.

It is with idioms, however, that he achieves his greatest flights. He slides off an expression and thinks he's gotten off a *bon mot* which is, in fact, just one more idiomatic leap in the soup from which George has been unable to rescue him. For him, one is "thrown out with a flea upon the ear," friction causes "the fur to jump about," "the dripping will be in the fire," "you have taken up a mare's nest," and a gentleman was "not born the preceding day."

The number of years in England have worked no more change on his mentality than on his appearance or hazardous control of English. Not for him the affectations of silliness or simple-mindedness, the casual or homey techniques of his pale-to-transparent English counterparts. Poirot bears little resemblance to the Campions and Wimseys, whose eccentricity is more a matter of absences than presences. They pride themselves on appearing addled; he cannot have too many compliments on a brain whose buzzing would put a bee out of business. It is their want of color, even physically, their lack of conceit, their apparent simplicity that causes them to flitter, so many horrid ghosts, across the pages. Their eccentricities float on a vagueness that is the exact opposite of the meticulous, methodical, precise Poirot whose mustaches, even in their flamboyance, are symmetrical.

Even the more vigorous police models, such as Appleby and Alleyn, stroll through a book protectively colored by tweeds, pipe smoke, and a sense of humor. Applying an observation of Chesterton on the mentality of French versus English writers to detectives, we might say, Poirot is very French in his rigid relevancy; Wimsey is very English in his rich irrelevance.

Because he is not English, Poirot can bypass a certain

number of cumbersome scruples no aristocratic or police detective could. He is fully capable of mimicking the hunt-and-peck school of detection, crawling on his hands and knees to look for clues, tracing footprints, and triumphantly bringing his thumb-print album to the dinner table. Nor is he above applying his ear to a crack in the door or slowing down to a halt when he hears a conversation of interest going forward on the other side of the hedge. His feelings about lying are that if one is to tell a lie, the more artful and elaborate the better.

Putting his theory into practice, Poirot invents ruses or relatives with equal ingenuity. His art is so refined the suspicion arises that, like the murderer, he would not take a straight path if he could invent a crooked one. Even in questioning, he circumnavigates, beginning with people least related to the crime, the estate agent who had the murder house to let, the village folks' gossip and opinions, even before approaching the servants.

Method and order are Poirot's dogma. Instinct and intuition, anathema. The mind without order cannot hope to arrive at the correct solution. One must not allow oneself to get drawn off into side issues. Opinions must never be mistaken for facts.

Once a sufficient number of facts have been gathered, and seem as snarled and contradictory as a tangled ball of yarn, it is time for Poirot to say, *"Voilà!"* He sees the light. He does not know who the murderer is, but he knows the nature of the crime. This is the turning point. Now, it is only necessary, like the prince with Cinderella's slipper, to find the criminal to fit the crime. The moment, in fact, of the Little Gray Cells.

What do the Little Gray Cells tell us? If we are clever, they tell us the psychology of the murder. We eliminate, then, not by clues and alibis, but by character. What kind of person must the murderer have been to commit the type of crime? Was it a man or a woman? A simple or a shrewd person?

If the total performance is as mechanical as the wind-up

doll his looks so admirably entitle him to be; if it seems he might be tumbled in a washing machine and step out impeccable and undaunted as ever, M. Poirot would exclaim, "*Mais, c'est entendu!* That is part of the method. Not to be confused by emotion." As he says, with obvious relief, "*Dieu merci,* I am not of ardent temperament."

Voilà, Hercule Poirot, the original egghead, originator of the method of the Little Gray Cells, detective *extraordinaire,* neither fact collector nor clue juggler, but psychologist of murder.

† GOURMET MEALS

The elaborate tastes and elegant ways of the distinguished detective—aristocratic or continental—require the most assiduous care; he is helpless without the sensitive ministrations of his man. While Poirot's George soothes his master's nerves with herbal *tisanes,* Bunter amuses Wimsey by gutting trout and washing potatoes under an outside tap on a holiday in Scotland, then turning about to receive casual visitors with proper West End ceremony. Stevens, the former butler in Agatha Christie's *The Seven Dials Mystery,* brings his young gentleman tea to wake him in the morning, and announces the presence of young ladies waiting in his sitting room. No proper gentleman's gentleman can ever be caught short by sudden guests or strange requests. The gentleman's gentleman is discreet, and thinks for him; he is expressionless, polite, incredibly intuitive, and johnny-on-the-spot when it comes to simple little repasts. At the drop of a calling card, the gentleman's gentleman can treat unexpected guests to an omelet followed by quails, and a fluff of a soufflé.

GOURMET MEALS

Celeriac Remoulade
Pâté de Campagne
Leek Pie
Lobster Soup
Mackerel with Fennel
Sole Véronique
Devonshire Sole
Turbot Hollandaise
Chicken Breasts in Brandy Cream
Chicken alla Porchetta
Apricot Duck
Tournedos with Foie Gras and Brandy
Beefsteak and Kidney Pie
Veal in Vermouth
Sweetbreads en Croûte
Potatoes Anna
Braised Celery
Baked Stuffed Zucchini
Onion Soufflé
Buttered Brussels Sprouts
Cold Cucumbers in Cream
Gooseberry Fool
Pêche Muscatel
Strawberry Soufflé with Raspberry-Almond Sauce
Crême Brulée
Greengage Plum Mousse
Poires Flambées
Rhubarb Charlotte

† CELERIAC REMOULADE
(4 servings)

2 knobs celeriac (celery root)	2 tbsp wine vinegar
2 tbsp mustard	⅛ tsp black pepper
½ tsp salt	½ cup olive oil

Peel and cut the celery root into thin, matchlike strips. Drop them in a kettle of boiling salted water, and boil 1 minute. Drain and plunge in cold water. Drain again thoroughly and pat dry with a towel. Place in a bowl. Put the mustard, salt, vinegar, and pepper in a blender. Spin and add the oil gradually. Pour the creamy mixture over the celery root and mix well. Cover and let stand in the refrigerator for several hours.

Note: white turnip makes an excellent substitute for the sometimes hard to find celeriac.

† PÂTÉ DE CAMPAGNE
(four servings)

1 lb boneless veal	¼ tsp allspice
1 lb boneless lean pork	pinch of thyme
½ lb pork fat	1 large bay leaf
2 eggs slightly beaten	½ lb pork liver
3 cloves garlic, pressed	½ cup dry white wine
½ cup cognac	½ lb slice of cooked ham,
2½ tsp salt	½ inch thick
½ tsp black pepper	¾ lb salt pork

Have the butcher grind the veal, pork, and pork fat finely together. Place in a nonmetal bowl. Combine the eggs, garlic, cognac, spices, and thyme, and mix well with the meat. Let stand at least 30 minutes.

Purée the pork liver and wine in a blender. Cube the ham in ½ inch cubes. Mix everything together very thoroughly. Cubed smoked tongue and pistachios may also be added at this point if desired.

Boil the salt pork in a large pan of water for 5 minutes. Rinse well and pat dry. Cut in very thin, long slices, and line the bottom and sides of a heatproof glass loaf pan with them.

Preheat the oven to 375° F. Fill the terrine with the meat mixture, smoothing it evenly on top. Halve the bay leaf and place the pieces on top. Cover the top with salt pork slices and finally with heavy aluminum foil. Place in a pan containing 3 inches of boiling water and bake for 1½ hours. Remove the foil and bake 30 minutes more. Take out both pans at once. Place another loaf tin, one that will fit inside the edges of the one containing the pâté, directly on the pâté. Fill it with some heavy object and let the fat spill into the larger pan containing the water. Leave at room temperature until thoroughly cooled. Still keeping the weights on, chill the pâté before serving. This may be served from the terrine. If it is going to be entirely consumed it may be turned out on a platter with the fat removed and decorated with aspic or with sprigs of parsley.

† *LEEK PIE*
(4 servings)

Savory Pie Crust (page 261)	chicken bouillon
6 to 8 leeks	2 tbsp heavy cream
6 tbsp diced Canadian bacon	2 eggs
½ bay leaf	

Make the pastry and let it rest. Cut off the green part of the leeks. Wash the leeks thoroughly and dice them. Throw the diced bacon in boiling water and cook 2 minutes. Drain and rinse in cold water. Put the leeks, bacon, and bay leaf in a pan and just cover with chicken bouillon. Simmer very slowly until almost dry. Take off the heat and remove the bay leaf.

Preheat the oven to 425° F.

Blend the cream with 1 egg and slowly pour the mixture into the pan, stirring constantly. Spread the mixture in a pie plate. Roll out the pastry quite thin and cover the pie plate, trimming the edges and pressing them firmly to the rim. Beat the remaining egg until just blended and brush the pastry twice over with it. Make a few slits in the pastry to let the steam escape and bake 15 minutes.

† *LOBSTER SOUP*
(4 servings)

1 carrot	3 tbsp butter
1 onion	3 tbsp flour
few celery leaves	2 cups milk
pinch of thyme	¼ cup sherry
¼ bay leaf	1 tsp lemon juice
1 cup dry white wine	red coloring (optional)
2 quarts water	1 cup cream
1½ tsp salt	salt and pepper
2 live chicken lobsters	cayenne
	chopped parsley

Cut the vegetables into chunks and place them along with the celery leaves, herbs, white wine, water, and salt in a kettle. Cover and simmer for 15 minutes. Add the lobsters. Bring to a boil and cook over moderate heat for 15 minutes. Turn off the heat and remove the lobsters. Rinse them in cold water, crack the claw shells and break off the tail. Take out the meat and extract the stomach, tomale (liver), and coral (roe) if any. Reserve the coral. Throw the shells back into the kettle and boil down the liquid until it measures about 3 cups. Sauté the coral lightly in 1 tsp butter in a small skillet.

Remove the black strip from the middle of the tail meat, and cut all the meat into small dice, saving a little for a garnish. Heat the butter and sauté the diced meat over moderate heat for 2 minutes, stirring so that the lobster is well coated with the butter. Sprinkle with the flour and continue stirring until the flour disappears. Add 1 cup of milk and stir until well blended. Add the remaining milk and continue stirring until thick. Strain the boiled-down liquor in which the lobsters were cooked and pour it into the soup, stirring until smooth. Add the sherry and lemon juice and a few drops of red coloring to give a rosy hue to the soup. If you have the coral, rub it through a sieve and add it. Cover and simmer for 10 minutes. Add the cream and season to taste with salt, pepper, and a little cayenne. Reheat but do not boil. Serve in individual bowls garnished with diced lobster and chopped parsley.

† MACKEREL WITH FENNEL
(4 servings)

4 1-lb mackerels	½ cup fine bread crumbs
olive oil	1 tbsp chopped parsley
1 large onion, chopped fine	lemon wedges
3 tbsp chopped fennel	
salt and pepper	
2 tsp lemon juice	

Cut off the heads of the mackerel. Slit them down the belly and clean them, removing the backbone. Wash and pat dry with toweling. Open them up flat and make several incisions in the skin with a sharp knife.

Heat 2 tbsp olive oil in a small skillet and cook the onions until soft. Add the fennel and continue cooking until the onions are golden brown. Season with salt and pepper and spread in the bottom of a shallow heatproof serving dish. Lay the mackerel on the vegetables. Sprinkle with lemon juice, salt and pepper and a layer of bread crumbs. Sprinkle generously with olive oil and bake 15 minutes at 425° F. Garnish with chopped parsley and lemon wedges.

† SOLE VÉRONIQUE

1½ cups seedless white grapes	1½ tbsp soft butter
1 cup dry white wine	1½ tbsp flour
1 small onion, minced	¼ cup milk
1½ tbsp butter	½ cup cream
3 lbs fillet of sole	1 tsp lemon juice
salt and pepper	
½ cup water	

Bring the grapes just to a boil in the white wine. Set aside. Cook the onion in a small pan in butter until soft. Spread the minced onion on the bottom of a shallow baking dish and lay the fillets on top of the onion. Season with salt and pepper and drain the white wine from the grapes over the fish. Add the water. Cover with buttered aluminum foil and bring to a simmer on top of the stove. Simmer very gently for 10 minutes or until the fish is flaky and tender. Carefully drain all the liquid into a saucepan without disturbing the fish. Boil down the liquid until it measures 1 cup. Keep the fish warm.

Meanwhile mix the butter and flour into a paste. Drop bits of the flour mixture into the sauce, whisking it until it is smooth. Add the milk, cream, and lemon juice and season to taste. Reheat but do not boil. Pour the sauce over the fish and brown lightly under a preheated broiler. Garnish with the grapes.

† DEVONSHIRE SOLE
(4 servings)

Devonshire sole is a lovely combination of sole, soft roes, and lobster sauce. If you are fortunate your dealer will supply you with both the sole and the roes, but if the roe is not available, substitute canned shad roe.

4 large sole fillets	2 tbsp sherry
4 soft roes	lemon juice
salt and pepper	chopped parsley
flour	
5 tbsp butter	
½ lb lobster	
¾ cup heavy cream	

Sprinkle the fish and roes with salt and pepper and dip them lightly in flour. Set aside for a moment.

Heat 2 tbsp butter in a small skillet and sauté the lobster meat over moderate heat, stirring so that the lobster is coated on all sides. Sprinkle with 1 tbsp flour and stir until the flour disappears. Add the cream and sherry and reheat but do not boil. Taste for seasoning.

Heat 3 tbsp butter in a large skillet and fry the fish for 4 to 5 minutes on each side depending on the thickness. Place the fillets on a heated platter and quickly sauté the roes in the same butter. Place a roe on each fillet and sprinkle with lemon juice and chopped parsley. Surround the fish with the lobster sauce. Serve with small potato balls cooked in butter.

† TURBOT HOLLANDAISE
(4 servings)

Fortunately, flash-frozen turbot is now available in markets in many parts of the country and while this does not equal the fresh variety found in the Pacific and on the other side of the Atlantic, it is very good. Substitute fresh flounder or sole if turbot is not to be found.

2 lbs turbot	HOLLANDAISE
1 cup milk	3 egg yolks
2 tsp grated onion	3 tbsp cream or evaporated milk
1 tsp salt	4 tsp lemon juice
	6 tbsp butter
	salt
	cayenne

Thaw frozen fish just before cooking. Place the turbot in a deep skillet with the milk, onion, salt, and enough water to just cover the fish. Bring slowly to a boil and simmer 10 to 15 minutes or until the fish flakes when pierced with a fork.

Meanwhile, whisk the egg yolks, cream, and lemon juice vigorously and ceaselessly in a saucepan over moderate heat until the sauce thickens. Remove from the heat and beat in the butter, 2 tbsp at a time. It's good to have someone nearby with the butter so that you won't have to stop beating. Season with salt and cayenne to taste.

Transfer the fish with two spatulas to a heated platter. If too moist pat it dry with a clean towel before spreading a little Hollandaise over the fish. Serve the rest in a separate bowl and accompany the dish with boiled potatoes.

† *CHICKEN BREASTS IN BRANDY CREAM*
(4 servings)

2 large chicken breasts, halved	2 egg yolks light beaten
salt and pepper	2 tsp lemon juice
8 tbsp butter	2 tbsp brandy
1 pint heavy cream	chopped parsley

Wash and dry the breasts of chicken and sprinkle them with salt and pepper. Heat 4 tbsp butter in a heavy skillet or electric frying pan. Brown the breasts on both sides over moderate heat. Do not burn the butter. Add the rest of the butter. Cover and simmer 45 minutes, turning occasionally. Add the cream and simmer 5 minutes longer.

Transfer the chicken to a heated platter and keep warm. Quickly boil down by half the contents of the pan, scraping the juices from the bottom and stirring. Remove from the heat and pour in a combination of the egg yolks, lemon juice, and brandy, stirring until well blended. Season with salt and pepper. Pour over the chicken and sprinkle with chopped parsley. Serve with Fluffy Rice (page 260).

† *CHICKEN ALLA PORCHETTA*
(4 servings)

1 3½ lb roasting chicken	¼ lb prosciutto
1 tbsp olive oil	1 fresh fennel bulb, sliced thin
freshly ground pepper	2 twigs dried fennel

Rub the chicken inside and out with olive oil and pepper. Insert two finger-sized rolls of prosciutto and 3 slices of fresh fennel in the cavity. Grease a casserole dish with olive oil, lay twigs of dried fennel on the bottom and put the chicken on them. Place the remaining fresh fennel around the chicken, cover and cook in a 400° F oven for 1¼ hours or until tender.

† *APRICOT DUCK*
  (4 servings)

1 4½ lb duck	1 lb can apricot halves
salt and pepper	1 orange
½ lemon	1 lemon
¼ cup apricot jam	2 tbsp Cointreau
1 cup dry white wine	watercress
1 tsp cornstarch	

Remove as much fat as possible from the cavity and neck end of the duck. Cut off the wings and neck. Sprinkle the inside with salt and pepper. Bind the legs to the body with a skewer or with kitchen twine. Prick the skin with a fork in several places to let the fat run out while cooking. Rub with the cut side of the half lemon and place on a rack in a roasting pan.

Roast the duck 1½ hours in a 350° F oven, removing the fat from the pan every 30 minutes with a syringe baster. Halfway through the roasting, turn the duck over to brown the back. At the end of the cooking period, turn the duck over again, sprinkle with salt and pepper, and brush with apricot jam. Return to the oven for 10 minutes. While the duck cooks, boil the neck, wings and gizzard in water and reduce to about a cup of broth.

Place the duck on a heated platter and pour off the fat from the roasting pan. Add the wine and cook over moderate heat, scraping up the juices adhering to the pan. Add the cornstarch dissolved in a little water, and the broth made from boiling the neck, wings, and gizzard. Stir and boil for 2 or 3 minutes.

Spin ½ cup of the apricot halves in a blender. Add ¼ cup of orange juice, the finely grated rinds of the orange and lemon, 1 tsp lemon juice, and the Cointreau. Mix this into the gravy in the roasting pan, bring to a boil and pour into a gravy boat. Garnish the duck with apricot halves and watercress.

† *TOURNEDOS WITH FOIE GRAS AND BRANDY*
(4 servings)

This is expensive but delicious. Tournedos are small steaks approximately 3 inches in diameter and 1¼ inches thick, cut from the tenderloin. The steaks are wrapped around the edges in pork fat tied securely with a string. If your butcher is not knowledgeable, buy 1¼ lbs tenderloin and ¼ lb salt port cut long (1″ x 6″) and achieve them yourself, making sure that the salt pork is freshened by boiling and sliced very thin.

4 tournedos	4 slices ¼ inch thick firm
1 small can truffled foie gras	bread cut in rounds
4 tbsp brandy	3 tbsp chopped parsley
¾ cup canned bouillon	2 tbsp oil
6 tbsp butter	salt and pepper

Wipe the steaks dry. Cut the foie gras into 4 slices. Place the slices in a small dish with 1 tbsp brandy and ¼ cup of the bouillon. Heat in a slow oven or over boiling water for a few minutes or until just warm.

Heat 2 tbsp butter in a skillet until very hot, and brown the rounds of bread which should be a little larger than the steaks. Brown on both sides, and sprinkle the edges with the chopped parsley to coat them well. Place on a platter and keep warm.

Add 2 tbsp oil and 2 more tbsp butter to the same skillet and, when sizzling hot, brown the steaks for 3 minutes, turn, sprinkle with salt and pepper and cook 3 minutes more. Pour the excess fat from the pan. With the steaks still in the pan, pour the rest of the brandy over them and ignite it. Spoon the sauce over the steaks until the flames are extinguished. Remove the string and fat from the steaks and put on the toast rounds. Add the rest of the bouillon to the pan and boil it down to a glaze, stirring with a fork to blend all the juices. Add 2 more tbsp butter and spoon the sauce over the steaks. Top with the slices of foie gras. Serve with shoe-string potatoes and fresh asparagus.

† *BEEFSTEAK AND KIDNEY PIE*
(4 servings)

Savory Pie Pastry (see page 261)   flour
2 lbs steak (rump or top round)   1 egg yolk
salt and pepper   1 can gelatinized beef
1 tbsp chopped parsley   consommé
2 shallots, finely chopped
1 veal kidney

Make the pastry and let it rest in the refrigerator. Order the steak cut 1½ inches thick. Slice it in thin, uniform pieces, 2½ to 3 inches long. Lay the pieces in a row and, using a rolling pin, flatten them slightly. Sprinkle with salt, pepper, parsley, and shallots.

Remove the film and fatty core from the kidney and cut it in small pieces. Place a piece of kidney on each slice of steak and roll it up. Dip each roll in flour seasoned with salt and pepper, and place them, seam side down, loosely in a shallow 2 quart casserole. The center of the heap should be somewhat higher than the rim of the dish. Fill ¾ full with cold water.

Preheat the oven to 425° F.

Roll out the pastry into a circle 1½ inches wider than the diameter of the casserole. Cut off a strip 1 inch wide around the edge and place it around the rim of the casserole. Moisten it and then lay the top crust over the whole dish, pinching the edges together and turning them up slightly. Any remaining pastry can be cut into decorative shapes, moistened and placed on the pastry. Cut a ½ inch hole in the center to let the steam escape. Brush with the beaten egg yolk. Bake ½ hour. Reduce the heat to 350° F. Cover the pastry with moistened, brown paper and continue to bake for 1½ hours. Remove the pie and pour in enough hot consommé to fill the casserole. This may be served hot or cold.

† VEAL IN VERMOUTH
(4 servings)

4 large veal chops, 1 inch thick	2 tbsp chopped parsley
2 tbsp oil	salt and pepper
4 tbsp butter	½ cup dry white vermouth
1 carrot, grated	½ pint sour cream
1 onion, grated	noodles

Wipe the chops dry. Heat the oil and 2 tbsp butter in a large skillet. When sizzling hot, brown the chops 3 minutes on each side and set them aside. Pour off the fat and add 2 tbsp butter to the skillet. Reduce the heat and cook the grated vegetables and parsley over moderate heat until very soft. Sprinkle with salt and pepper. Place the chops on the vegetables. Season with salt and pepper and add ¼ cup of vermouth. Cover and simmer 20 minutes.

Remove the chops to a heated platter and keep warm. Turn up the heat and add ¼ cup more vermouth, stirring vigorously to loosen any juices adhering to the pan. Stir in the sour cream and heat, but do not boil. Pour the sauce over the chops and surround them with a ring of buttered noodles.

† SWEETBREADS EN CROÛTE
(4 servings)

This is made in stages. It is well to start a day in advance.

SAVORY PASTRY	1 cup chicken broth
2 lbs sweetbreads, fresh	½ cup dry white wine
or frozen	1 bay leaf
1 large onion	2 sprigs parsley
2 carrots	¼ tsp thyme
2 stalks celery	1 tsp tomato paste
6 tbsp butter	1 cup heavy cream
½ lb small mushrooms	½ lemon
flour	1 egg yolk
salt and white pepper	

Make a double recipe of Savory Pie Pastry (page 261) or buy frozen flaky pastry which is in the market and is very satisfactory and easy to roll out.

Soak the sweetbreads 2 to 3 hours in cold water. Remove the filament and any blood clots.

Dice the onion, carrots, and celery. Cook them in 2 tbsp butter in a large skillet until soft. Remove them with a slotted spoon to a heat-proof casserole and spread them over the bottom. Wash and dry the mushrooms, using only the caps. Sauté them in 2 tbsp butter, using the same skillet. When the mushrooms are almost dry, remove them from the skillet and set aside for future use.

Dry the sweetbreads with toweling. Coat lightly with flour and season with salt and white pepper. Heat the remaining butter in the skillet and brown the sweetbreads 2 to 3 minutes on each side. Transfer them to the casserole. Add the broth, wine, and herbs. Bring just to a boil on top of the stove, then transfer the casserole to a 300° F oven, place on a lower rack, and cook 40 minutes.

Put the sweetbreads on a large plate. Do not worry if they separate into lobes. Cover with another plate and weight it down with some heavy object. Strain the cooking broth and set aside to cool.

The next day, roll out the pastry in a rectangle large enough to envelop the sweetbreads. Spread with a thin film of butter. Stand the sections of sweetbreads one against the other so that they form something like a small roast. Wrap the pastry around them. Trim off the ends, leaving enough to fold over and close the end openings. Place seam side down on a lightly buttered baking sheet. Cut out little flowers, leaves, or other designs from the remaining pastry and affix them with a little water to the crust in whatever design suits your fancy. Place this creation in the refrigerator until just before baking.

SAUCE: Remove the fat from the top of the cooking broth. Heat it in the top part of a double boiler with the mushrooms, tomato paste, and cream. Add the lemon juice and salt and pepper if necessary.

Preheat the oven to 450° F. Brush the pastry over twice with the egg yolk blended with 1 tsp water. Bake 20 to 25 minutes or until nicely browned. Transfer to a hot platter and surround the bottom with the sauce.

† *POTATOES ANNA*
(4 servings)

2 lbs new potatoes	salt and pepper
¼ lb soft butter	chopped parsley

Peel potatoes of approximately the same size and shape and slice them very thin. Soak the slices in cold water for an hour or more. Drain. Spread out a towel and pat them dry. Liberally butter the bottom and sides of a small, deep, round casserole dish with a cover or a charlotte mold. Line the bottom and sides with overlapping slices of potato. Smear the bottom layer with butter and season with salt and pepper. Over this put another tightly packed layer of potato slices. Continue this process until you have five or six layers of potatoes. Cover the final layer with a piece of buttered paper and put on a tightly fitting cover, or a double layer of aluminum foil. Bake 40 minutes at 400° F in the lower shelf of the oven.

Turn the cake out onto a heated platter and sprinkle with chopped parsley.

† *BRAISED CELERY*
(4 servings)

2 large celery hearts	⅛ tsp thyme
1 carrot, grated	½ bay leaf
1 onion, grated	salt and pepper
1 clove garlic, pressed	½ cups dry white wine
2 tbsp butter	1½ cups chicken broth
	2 tsp chopped parsley

Remove the outer stalks and the tops of the celery, leaving them 5 to 6 inches long. Cut them in half lengthwise and wash very carefully. Boil the celery in salted water for 12 minutes.

Meanwhile cook the carrot, onion, and garlic in butter in a shallow serving casserole. Stir in the thyme and bay leaf, and season with salt and pepper. Drain the celery thoroughly and place on top of the onion mixture. Add the white wine and just enough well-seasoned broth to come to the level of the celery. Cover with a round of buttered aluminum foil and bake 1 hour at 325° F, removing the foil for the last 15 minutes of cooking. Sprinkle with chopped parsley and serve from the dish.

† BAKED STUFFED ZUCCHINI
(4 servings)

8 zucchini, 4 to 5 inches long	1 tsp tomato paste
2 tbsp olive oil	2 tsp chopped basil
¼ cup shredded onion	3 tbsp dry vermouth
1 clove garlic, pressed	1 cup cooked rice
2 tbsp chopped parsley	4 tbsp Parmesan cheese, grated
½ cup pine nuts or chopped walnuts	salt and pepper
	butter

Choose zucchini of equal length. Since they are small, allow 2 per person. Trim the ends and wipe them clean. Drop into a kettle of boiling salted water, and cook 8 minutes. Drain and plunge in cold water. Divide them in half lengthwise and with a sharp pointed spoon, scoop out the seeds, leaving a deep enough cavity to hold the stuffing.

Heat the oil in a skillet and cook the onion, garlic, parsley, and pine nuts until the onions are soft. Add the tomato paste, basil, and vermouth. Stir well and mix with the rice, 2 tbsp grated Parmesan cheese, and season with salt and pepper.

Preheat the oven to 350° F.

Stuff the zucchinis with the mixture and place them in a buttered, heatproof serving dish. Dot with butter and sprinkle with more grated cheese. Bake 25 minutes.

† *ONION SOUFFLÉ*
(4 servings)

3 tbsp butter	3 egg yolks
¾ cups shredded onion	salt and pepper
¼ cup shredded carrot	pinch of nutmeg
3 tbsp flour	4 egg whites
1 cup rich milk	Parmesan cheese, grated

Heat the butter in a saucepan and cook the onion and carrot in it until the onion is soft. Sprinkle with flour and cook two minutes without browning. Add the milk and stir until it thickens. Beat the egg yolks well and, taking the pan off the heat, stir them in. Cook over low heat for 1 minute. Season highly with salt, pepper, and a little nutmeg. Cool.

Forty minutes before serving, preheat the oven to 350° F. Fold into the onion mixture the stiffly beaten egg whites. Put in a souffle dish liberally buttered and coated with Parmesan cheese. Bake 25 to 30 minutes. Ten minutes before the end of the cooking time, sprinkle the top with more cheese.

† *BUTTERED BRUSSELS SPROUTS*
(4 servings)

2 lbs (1½ quarts) Brussels sprouts	salt and pepper
5 tbsp butter	Parmesan cheese (optional)

Remove the wilted leaves from the outside of the sprouts and make a gash in each stem. Drop into a large kettle of boiling salted water and cook 10 to 15 minutes or until just tender. Do not overcook. Drain very thoroughly, squeezing out excess water very gently with the back of a large spoon.

Heat the butter in a large skillet, and toss the sprouts in the butter until well coated. Season well with salt and freshly ground black pepper. Place in a heated vegetable dish and sprinkle with the grated cheese, or serve plain.

† COLD CUCUMBERS IN CREAM
(4 servings)

2 cucumbers	½ cup sour cream
½ tsp salt	½ cup heavy sweet cream
¼ tsp black pepper	3 tbsp vinegar
	1 tbsp chopped parsley

Peel the cucumbers unless they are fresh from the garden. Halve them and scoop out the seeds. Slice thin. Mix with the remaining ingredients and chill before serving.

† GOOSEBERRY FOOL
(4 servings)

1 quart gooseberries	½ cup sugar
	2 cups heavy cream, whipped

Remove the tops and tails from the berries and place them in a pan with the sugar and just enough water to cover. Boil until soft, and spin in a blender or force through a fine sieve. Cool.

Fold in the whipped cream and serve very cold in individual dessert glasses.

† *PÊCHE MUSCATEL*
(4 servings)

1 lb can finest quality peaches	1 cup muscatel wine
4 egg yolks	1 pint vanilla ice cream
3 tbsp sugar	toasted slivered almonds

Remove the peaches from the can and chill them in the refrigerator. Just before serving, beat the egg yolks, sugar, and wine in the top part of a double boiler over boiling water until the mixture begins to rise. Remove from the heat. Place chilled peach halves in stemmed dessert glasses, allowing 2 per serving. Top with a scoop of ice cream and cover with the warm sauce. Sprinkle with the slivered almonds and serve immediately. A helping hand is very useful in serving this dessert quickly.

† *STRAWBERRY SOUFFLÉ WITH RASPBERRY-ALMOND SAUCE*
(4 servings)

1 lb package frozen strawberries	1 tbsp gelatine
1 10-oz package frozen raspberries	½ cup cold water
6 tbsp confectioners' sugar	3 egg whites beaten stiff
3 egg yolks	⅛ tsp salt
1 lemon	½ pint heavy cream
½ cup sugar	slivered almonds

Put a 1½ inch paper collar around the top of a 1 quart soufflé dish, securing it in place with Scotch tape. Chill the dish in the refrigerator.

Spin the thawed strawberries in a blender and measure out 1¼ cups. Add the raspberries to the remaining strawberries and purée them, adding the confectioners' sugar gradually. Strain the purée into a small bowl. This is the sauce.

Combine the egg yolks, the grated rind and juice of the lemon, and sugar in the top part of a double boiler. Beat with an electric hand beater or a wire whisk over boiling water until doubled in volume. Soak the gelatine in cold water for 5 minutes. Remove the egg mixture from the heat and stir in the gelatine and the 1¼ cups of blended strawberries. Fill a bowl with ice and place the pan in it. Stir until the mixture thickens.

Beat the egg whites with the salt until very stiff. In another bowl beat the cream stiff. Fold small amounts of egg whites and cream alternately into the strawberry mixture. Pile it into the soufflé dish, letting it come to the top of the collar. Chill in the refrigerator several hours.

To serve: Remove the paper collar and spread the top with a little of the raspberry sauce and sprinkle with almonds. Serve the rest of the sauce in a small sauce bowl.

† *CRÈME BRULÉE*
(4 servings)

1 pint heavy cream	⅛ tsp salt
4 egg yolks	1½ tsp vanilla
¼ cup sugar	light brown sugar

Preheat the oven to 325° F. Scald the cream without letting it boil. Beat the egg yolks, white sugar, salt and vanilla until light and creamy. Add the hot cream gradually, beating constantly. Pour into a shallow 8 or 9 inch baking dish, place it in a pan of hot water, and bake on the middle rack of oven for 30 to 35 minutes, or until an inserted silver knife comes out clean. Cool and then chill in the refrigerator.

Preheat the broiler. Place the crème in a pan of ice. Spread the top with a layer of brown sugar. Place under the broiler just long enough to melt the sugar. Serve immediately, or chill again in the refrigerator.

† *GREENGAGE PLUM MOUSSE*
(4 servings)

3 egg yolks	12 oz jar greengage preserves
1 cup heavy cream	1 tbsp lemon juice
1 tsp vanilla extract	few drops green coloring
	3 egg whites, beaten stiff

Cook the slightly beaten egg yolks and the cream over low heat. Keep the mixture just below the boiling point and stir constantly until the mixture is thick and coats the sides of the pan. This will take about 5 minutes. Remove from the heat and add the vanilla, greengage preserves, lemon juice, and coloring. Mix thoroughly. Place in a chilled ice tray and put in the freezing compartment of the refrigerator for 45 minutes.

Chill the bowl and beater of an electric beater. Beat the egg whites stiff in another bowl. Quickly beat the frozen mixture in the chilled bowl until it is smooth. Fold in the egg whites and refreeze for 2 to 3 hours.

† *POIRES FLAMBÉES*

1 30-oz can pears in heavy syrup	⅓ cup Cointreau
8 large candied cherries	⅓ cup brandy
1 tsp arrowroot or cornstarch	

Place the drained pears in a lightly buttered, heatproof dish or in a chafing dish. Place a cherry in each cavity. Combine one cup of the syrup with the arrowroot or cornstarch and whisk until blended. Bring the syrup to a boil, remove from the heat, and add the Cointreau. Pour over the pears. Just before serving, reheat. Heat the brandy, sprinkle it over the pears and ignite it.

† *RHUBARB CHARLOTTE*
(4 servings)

1 lb rhubarb	6 to 8 slices firm white bread
2 tbsp grated orange rind	¼ lb butter
⅔ cup sugar	½ pint heavy cream

Wash the rhubarb and cut in 1 inch lengths. Combine with the orange rind and sugar in the top of a double boiler. Cover and cook over boiling water until the rhubarb is tender and the mixture is thick. Cool.

Preheat the oven to 375° F. Trim the crusts off the bread. Cut two of the slices the size and shape of the bottom of a small charlotte mold or soufflé dish. Cut the rest into strips 1½ inches wide and the height of the dish. Melt the butter. Dip one of the rounds in the butter and place it in the bottom of the dish. Dip the strips in the butter and line the sides of the dish, overlapping the strips slightly. Fill with the rhubarb mixture and cover with the remaining round dipped in butter. Press firmly into place. Bake in the lower third of the oven for 30 minutes. Remove from the oven and let stand 5 minutes. Loosen the edges with a knife and turn out onto a dessert platter. Serve with heavy cream.

THIRTY-SIX

Witness for Wittiness

Suddenly, with a great *plop!* the bog let go its hold. . . .

"What a beastly place," said Lord Peter faintly. "'Pologise, stupid of me to have forgotten—what'sy name?"

"Well, tha's loocky," said one of their rescuers. "We thowt we heerd someun a-shouting. There be few folks as cooms oot o' Peter's Pot dead or alive, I reckon."

"Well, it was nearly potted Peter that time," said his lordship, and fainted.

DOROTHY L. SAYERS, *Clouds of Witness*

Wit in the mystery is another standard flapping from the castle turret signifying urbanity is in residence, polish is undimmed, aplomb is ours; that as long as there's an England or an us— though wind or war rattle at the windows, and murder hammer at the door—whisky glasses will clink, the cretonne fade, and the drawing room comedy go on. Wit assures us we are participating in a civilized world of elegance, sophistication, and ease, and that in that world we are untouched by pain. We may refuse, as we would cut a cad at a dinner party, to acknowledge it. In such a world, we are always masters of ourselves and the situation, not swept to and fro by circumstances, but standing—with the aristocratic detective—aloof, smiling slightly, and in control. Here, even murder is without the power to threaten us, and could not conceivably make us less happy or gay.

Wit, as distinct from humor, which can cross class lines, is the sole property of the upper classes. All humor requires us to see a situation as observers. Wit goes further, requiring more than visual, verbal, or even emotional recognition, but a detached and intellectual sprightliness that delves into its cupboard full of erudite snippets, and brings them brightly to bear on apparently diverse subjects, often at particularly tight moments.

Presumably, wit comes on at Eton, where it is passed from one young noble hand to another, relay fashion, some time after the mumps, and gains polish with rooms, sherry in the afternoon, and coming down from Oxford or Cambridge. Those who remain, i.e., the dons, close as they are to the storehouses of knowledge, perfect it utterly but, unfortunately, the hard, dry quality wit must have is inclined, when confined too long behind the walls of academia, to crumble like an artifact on exposure to air. Wit, without the leveling influence of worldly contact, lends itself too readily to pedantry.

It is up to the aristocratic detective, coming down from Oxford, to carry the standard. He is generally better equipped to keep his wits than the victims of the crime, who may have lost some of their detachment along about the second body. As opposed to dons *(sic transit gloria mundi)*, the detective's refinements have met with some worldly buffeting, so if a poetic allusion or Latin phrase drops with his monocle, it may be comprehensible.

Recognizing sources is a subgame in a mystery, second only, in difficulty and delight, to recognizing clues. But, as *Alice's*

Adventures in Wonderland is a veritable concordance for a number of authors, if the reader is up on his *Alice,* and has chanced on Shakespeare, he will manage a flattering number of witticisms. If he does not, it won't matter any more than missing a nuance or two in a Beethoven string quartet. There are always more where they came from.

Police rarely have wit; maids never do. It may be they have nothing to laugh about. Peers find poverty itself rather amusing —if not carried too far. It's all right as long as they can buy second cars to spare the Rolls, treat their wives to champagne dinner after they've popped their pearls, or holiday at some dreary little place like Monte Carlo on the Cote d'Azur. Being drummed out of the corps at the track, or not paying your bookmaker is carrying it too far.

Possibly, as part of their carefully cultivated detachment, the gentry develop an unequaled ability to laugh at themselves. Some are such merry old souls, as we learn in Ngaio Marsh's *Death of a Peer,* they can sit down to a dinner that runs all the way from soup to savories an hour and a half after locating an elder brother in the lift, his eye poised on the end of a skewer. A meal of this sort does not, of course, indicate appetite, but discipline-to-gaiety, otherwise known as form.

Wit is at home with the upper classes. The flexibility and trained brain, the kind of rapier flicks of fantasy wit requires are more liable to thrive on champagne and detachment than on scrubbing floors and weekly paychecks. In short, the upper-class mentality and atmosphere, where gaiety is not a spontaneous giggle, but a duty; not sparkle, but substance.

THIRTY-SEVEN

The Proof of the Pudding

The telephone bell rang. Poirot rose, glancing at his watch as he did so. The time was close on half-past eleven. He wondered who was ringing him up at this hour. It might, of course, be a wrong number.

"And it might," he murmured to himself with a whimsical smile, "be a millionaire newspaper proprietor, found dead in the library of his country house, with a spotted orchid in his left hand and a page torn from a cookery book pinned to his breast."

AGATHA CHRISTIE, "The Yellow Iris"

When the last fork has been laid on the plate, the last crumb of a treacle tart has been eaten, the last Admirable Eccentric has daubed his mustache with a starched white napkin and gotten up from the table, the case is definitely proved. Not against the murderer. For a way of life.

The case for thin slices of bread and butter with tea, and

drapes drawn, before rising in the morning. The case for a housemaid coming with a copper can of hot water to pour into a rose-patterned basin. The case for the sound of voices at breakfast coming from downstairs, and the prospect of sausages and chestnuts. The case for elevenses, if one merely wants to feel spoiled; for milk toast, if feeling fragile. The case for buttery muffins, grandmother's receipts, brandy for the fainting, meat pies for the police, curry for poisoning. For butlers serving breath-light soufflés, and solicitously bending over one's chair. For the soothing susurration of civilized conversation. For tea in the afternoon, fires in the grates and, no matter what the circumstances: "Dinner is served, Madam." For being strong, healthy, well-bred, and English.

We have been safely within the walls, enclosed behind the oak door, guarded by the sharp-voiced collie, looked after by our hostess, who has done everything in her power—seen to the scented linens, biscuits in the tin by the bed, the ebullient bouquets straining their vases—to make us forgetful of what is called reality. No untoward noise—except the murder cry—has escaped thick Turkey carpets or gently bred lips. No unnecessary thinking; our hostess and the servants have seen to that. No entertainment has been arranged, except what might most beguile us. We have been charmed by the assembled guests, the foibles of the staff, the darting wit of the detective, the amusing cloddishness of a police-inspector, the cooperative spirit of the victim, yet not one clever word or polite gesture have we had to add.

In fine, the mystery author has been the perfect hostess. Anticipating our needs, as does Lord Caterham's butler in Agatha Christie's *The Seven Dials Mystery*, "in the most marvellous manner," taking us well beyond our expectations—which only looked for escape, an idle weekend in the country, or the glitter of the city; a chance to be taken out of ourselves.

Instead, we have been taken past ourselves. Our minds, far

from turning off, have raced, run, reasoned, weighed, searched clues in sarcophagi with prying spinsters, shuffled alibis with indomitable detectives, poured over fingerprints with the police. In addition to all the ingredients of rest and relaxation, we have been offered the best treat (and treatment) of all, an invitation to a game—a game of the highest order—a game of life and death. In this game, we have exercised our faculties without the promise of prizes, but without the tension of having to win or lose; each playing, each winning, each of us having a good romp, and working up a tremendous appetite while we're about it.

In fact, our authors have done so well by us, it might seem there is nothing left to do. By the end of the book, we have lived the gentle life, but far from being stultified by the smooth abundance, it has been as buoying as champagne with a dash of bitters: murder. At every turn, we have encountered food. We have seen food set the scene, loosen the tongue, poison the benefactor, lure an innocent maid, settle the shattered, make everything real. We have sat down to sup with murderers, victims, and also-rans, vicariously enjoying their victuals, while vicariously trembling over their plights.

We have tasted, smelled, enjoyed—for all these can be done with the imagination. What remains is that final sensation in the stomach called satisfaction. The only thing we haven't done is eaten, really eaten. This, for all our authors' care, is up to us. Now, the moment is here to lay aside insubstantial forks from invisibly steaming food, seated at ectoplasmic tables, on fancied chairs, eating mental meals. The clues have brought us through apprehension, beyond doubt, past puzzle, by proof, to appetite. Real, full-blooded appetite. Answerable only by genuine, and genuinely delicious, food. There is nothing to do, but to step hastily into the kitchen, and serve it forth.

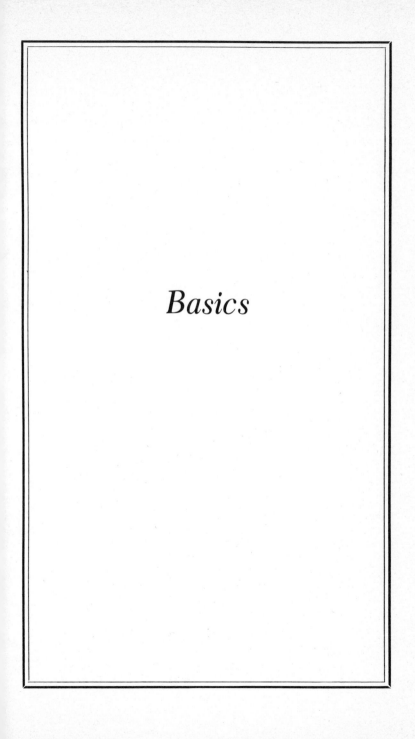

Basics

BASICS

White Sauce
Vinaigrette Sauce
Fluffy Rice
Savory Pie Pastry for Single Crust
Dessert Pastry for Tarts and Flans

† *WHITE SAUCE*

3 tbsp butter   1 tsp salt
4 tbsp flour   ⅛ tsp white pepper
2 cups milk

Heat the butter over low heat in a saucepan. Stir in the flour and cook slowly, stirring constantly, for 2 or 3 minutes. Increase the heat but do not let the butter and flour brown. Add half the milk and stir vigorously until blended. Add the rest of the milk and continue stirring until the mixture thickens. Season with salt and pepper.

† *VINAIGRETTE SAUCE*

¼ cup good wine vinegar   ⅛ tsp black pepper
½ tsp Dijon mustard   ½ cup peanut or salad oil
½ tsp salt   ¼ cup olive oil

Combine all the ingredients in a jar or bottle and shake until blended.

† *FLUFFY RICE*

Slowly pour 1 cup of long grain rice in a large pan of boiling salted water so that the water never ceases to boil. Stir once and boil 12 to 14 minutes or until the rice is just tender. Drain in a collander and run cold water through it immediately, fluffing the rice with a fork. Thirty minutes before serving bake in a lightly buttered covered dish in a 325° F oven. The result is 4 cups of perfect dry and fluffy rice.

† *DESSERT PASTRY FOR TARTS AND FLANS*

(FOR TWO CRUSTS)

2 cups all-purpose flour	2 tsp sugar
½ tsp salt	1 egg yolk
⅓ cup butter	3 tbsp ice water
⅓ cup vegetable shortening	

(FOR ONE CRUST)

1½ cups all-purpose flour	1½ tsp sugar
¼ tsp salt	1 egg yolk
5 tbsp butter	2 tbsp ice water
4 tbsp vegetable shortening	

Combine the flour and salt in a bowl. Cut the butter and shortening in with a pastry blender, 2 knives, or a single electric beater until the mixture is pebbly. Add the sugar, egg yolk, and water and mix quickly and deftly with your fingers to form a ball. Knead on a marble or other working surface just until the dough is smooth. Cover well and store in the refrigerator for at least 30 minutes before rolling out.

† SAVORY PIE PASTRY FOR SINGLE CRUST

1½ cups all-purpose flour   3 tbsp vegetable shortening
⅛ tsp salt   2 to 3 tbsp ice water
5 tbsp butter

Combine the flour and salt in a bowl. Cut in the butter and shortening, using a pastry blender, 2 knives, or a single electric beater. When the mixture has a pebbly consistency, rub it between your fingers until it has a finely grained texture. Add ice water gradually to make the dough just sticky enough to form a ball. Knead briefly until smooth and glossy. Cover and store in the refrigerator at least 30 minutes before rolling out.

Index

Index